THE BOOK OF THE SHULCHAN ARUCH

BOOKS FROM CLEMENS & BLAIR

— www.clemensandblair.com —

For My Legionnaires, by Corneliu Codreanu
Myth and Sun, by Martin Friedrich
Unmasking Anne Frank, by Ikuo Suzuki
Pan-Judah! Political Cartoons of Der Stürmer, by Robert Penman
Passovers of Blood, by Ariel Toaff
The Poisonous Mushroom, by Ernst Hiemer
On the Jews and Their Lies, by Martin Luther
Mein Kampf, by Adolf Hitler
Mein Kampf (Dual English-German edition), by Adolf Hitler
The Essential Mein Kampf, by Adolf Hitler
The Myth of the 20th Century, by Alfred Rosenberg

BOOKS BY THOMAS DALTON

— www.thomasdaltonphd.com —

The Steep Climb: Essays on the Jewish Question
Classic Essays on the Jewish Question: 1850 to 1945
Debating the Holocaust
The Holocaust: An Introduction
The Jewish Hand in the World Wars
Eternal Strangers: Critical Views of Jews and Judaism
Hitler on the Jews
Goebbels on the Jews
Streicher, Rosenberg, and the Jews: The Nuremberg Transcripts

THE BOOK OF THE SHULCHAN ARUCH

---

by
Erich Bischoff

Edited by
Thomas Dalton, PhD

A joint publication of

Clemens & Blair, LLC *and* Castle Hill Publishers
— 2023 —

A joint production of:
CLEMENS & BLAIR, LLC
CASTLE HILL PUBLISHERS

Clemens & Blair, LLC, is a non-profit educational publisher.
www.clemensandblair.com

Library of Congress Cataloging-in-Publication Data

Bischoff, Erich
The Book of the Shulchan Aruch

A new English translation from German of *Das Buch vom Schulchan Aruch* (1942; 4th ed.)

p. cm.
Includes bibliographical references

ISBN 979-8986-7250-86
(pbk.: alk. paper)

1. Judaism
2. Shulchan Aruch, the
3. Talmud, the

Printing number: 9 8 7 6 5 4 3 2 1

Printed in the United States of America on acid-free paper.

ACKNOWLEDGMENT

The editor would like to acknowledge the assistance of Ms. Mildred Grau in creating this new translation from the German original. Her efforts are greatly appreciated.

CONTENTS

FOREWORD

THOMAS DALTON

I would hazard to say, with no exaggeration, that the *Shulchan Aruch* is the most important book that no one has ever heard of—no one, that is, who is not Jewish. This book, which is so vital to the ethos and worldview of Jews everywhere, is almost literally unknown in the non-Jewish world, even among the highly educated. Astonishingly, not even the title is known. This is a remarkable situation, one that demands an explanation; hence the importance of the present volume.

The author, Erich Bischoff, has performed a remarkable service to all of humanity with his clear, thorough, and honest assessment of the *Shulchan Aruch*, a book that defines so much of what it means to be a Jew. Judaism has long been shrouded in mystery, with its strange customs, bizarre dress, and inscrutable and seemingly antagonist moral code. As such, Gentiles everywhere have never really known with whom they are dealing, and thus how to respond to the Jewish presence and Jewish actions. Bischoff's book offers, for the first time—and still today, some 90 years after its original publication—the only concise and complete analysis of the *Shulchan Aruch*. This is doubly valuable given that he was a non-Jewish German, a renowned scholar, and someone who was able to dig deeply into the massive corpus of Jewish writing to extract the most interesting and most relevant material. Today, the few books on the *Shulchan Aruch* are written by Jews, and thus we never get an objective and unbiased assessment of the moral precepts of this oriental religion. Bischoff has remedied this shortcoming, and we can be eternally grateful that he has.

Let me begin with a few words about the author. It will be brief because little is known of his life. He was born in Germany in 1867 and progressed rapidly through his schooling, eventually gaining a deep academic training in biblical history, Hebrew, and the history of Judaism. Already by 1890, at the age of 23, he had published his first book, *Prolegomena zu Dionysius Cato*. This was followed by another book the next year, *Die Juden und das Christenblut* ('The Jews and the Blood of

Christians'). Knowledge of his expertise spread in German society, and by 1900 he was serving as an expert witness in various legal trials, most involving charges of anti-Semitism by local Jewish groups against other writers or speakers.

All the while, he continued to publish important works: *Kabbalah* (1903), *The Koran* (1904), *Jesus and the Rabbis* (1905), *Elements of Kabbalah* (1913), *Babylonian Astrology* (1907), *Rabbinical Fables* (1922), *Blood in Jewish Literature* (1929)—and the present work, *Das Buch vom Schulchan Aruch* ('The Book of the Shulchan Aruch'), also originally in 1929. Bischoff died in 1936 at the age of 69.

Apart from this short biography, we get a better understanding of this man from his writing, especially *The Book of the Shulchan Aruch*, which contains many personal reflections and asides. Here we find someone with both academic insight and moral courage, a man who understands deeply his subject matter and also sees that it has an important role to play in contemporary European society. Bischoff was clearly concerned that the public had little understanding of the basic tenets of Judaism, and he felt it his duty to enlighten his fellow citizens regarding the (mostly) negative aspects of Jewish morality. Then as now, isolated passages from older Jewish writings—mostly the Talmud—were extracted and deployed by enemies of the Jews to great effect, though often without the necessary context. As it turned out, this context, in many cases, made for an even harsher critique than the anti-Semites could have imagined. Suffice it to say that German Jews were less than pleased when Bischoff's authoritative, contextualized, and learned critique appeared in print.

Judaism in Context

Bischoff does an excellent job of explaining the relevant aspects of the *Shulchan Aruch*, but the Talmud, for example, is only of peripheral interest for him, as is the larger contextual history of Judaism. Here, I want to lay some of the groundwork for the reader to make it easier to follow Bischoff's line of thinking and to more easily absorb the import of what he writes.

The history of the Jews goes back to very ancient times in the Middle East; as early as 1200 BC, we have a relic, the Merneptah Stele, which mentions "Israel" by name. Even earlier, circa 1350 BC, we have letters to Egyptian pharaoh Akhenaten that refer to a people called 'Habiru,' which some believe are Hebrews. And another stone engraving of 850 BC refers to "the House of David." All these suggest a distinct and identifiable Jewish people in the region around present-day Palestine since at least 1000 BC.

It was likely in these early days that the Jews formulated and circulated amongst themselves stories about the origins of their people, of the Earth, and of their god, Yahweh. Allegorical figures such as Adam and Eve, Noah, Abraham, Esau, Jacob, Isaac, Joseph, and Moses came to be formalized in Jewish myth, and their various stories came to embody certain key elements of Jewish thinking and the Jewish worldview. Eventually around 500 BC, scholars believe that the first five books of the Old Testament were first written down, as a collection of writings known as the 'Torah' or the 'Five Books of Moses.' Over the next few hundred years, assorted other stories of Jewish prophets and kings came to be codified in the other 35 (or so) books of the Old Testament. Thus, the entire OT—called the 'Tanakh' by Jews—was likely complete by around 200 BC. The oldest physical remains, incidentally, are the Dead Sea Scrolls, which contain parts of much of the OT, and were apparently written between 200 and 100 BC.

The entire OT is not a large amount of text; in current form, and depending on which books are included and how it is formatted, the full OT runs about 1,000 pages of English text. This was sufficient to document the stories and the prophets, but not enough to address the many complexities of everyday life—especially for a people who wanted to live according to "God's law." Much was there, but much more was left out, or only implied. Thus it fell to the Jewish learned men—equivalent to the present-day 'rabbi,' even though that title did not exist until around 0 AD—to comment on, and flesh out, the 'intended meaning' of the OT for all the various issues, problems, and questions of daily life. Therefore, likely from the earliest days, there came to be an "oral Torah," handed down orally through the generations, as a guide to everyday life and as a supplement to the "written Torah" of the first five books of the OT, and indeed to all of it.

The "oral Torah" survived 'orally' for hundreds of years, until the Roman invasion of Judea in 63 BC and the destruction of the Jerusalem Temple in 70 AD. Jewry was dispersed to the many nations surrounding

Judea, and as far as Europe, Asia, and Africa. Soon thereafter, and in the face of this diaspora, some Jews felt the need to write down the 'oral Torah' for the benefit of a dispersed Jewish people. The first was apparently Rabbi HaNasi, around 200 AD; his work came to be known as the *Mishnah* ('the study'). As soon as that was completed, other rabbis began to document their own reaction and commentaries on it; these writings were called the *Gemara* ('the completion'). By 350 AD, there were so many commentaries to the already-extensive Mishnah that Jewish scholars in Palestine pulled them all together into a single document called the *Talmud* ('the teaching'). This first collection—now called the 'Palestine Talmud'—was expanded even further in 500 AD in a document called the 'Babylonian Talmud.' This latter document remains, to this day, "the" Talmud of Judaism; it is the most complete documentation of the ethics, morals, and daily requirements of the Jewish people.

Needless to say, the Talmud is a vast set of writings, far larger than any encyclopedia. Today, one can buy an English translation of the entire document, but it runs to some 50 volumes, covering almost 9 linear feet of shelf space. Dual English-Hebrew editions can be found, running from 73 to an astounding 146 volumes. One could spend years reading the Talmud and only ever grasp a fraction of the whole.

All this set the stage for another prominent Jewish rabbi by the name of Joseph Karo. Born in Toledo, Spain in 1488, he was forced by political circumstances to move to Portugal, Morocco, and Istanbul, eventually settling in Safed (present-day Israel) around 1535, at the age of 47. By this time, he saw the need to address the vastness and complexity of the Talmud by simplifying and condensing its most important points, eliminating much that was no longer relevant. Thus he wrote a set of books called *Beit Yosef* (or *'Beth Yosef'*), which took him some 20 years to complete. Evidently believing that even this was too unwieldly, Karo then undertook to write another, even more condensed version; this he called the 'Set Table' or *Shulchan Aruch.*

The *Shulchan Aruch*

Karo began the *Shulchan Aruch* around 1545 and worked on it for 10 years, eventually completing the new book in 1555 when he was 67. It was not published for another 10 years, in 1565. Karo died in 1575 at the age of 87.

Meanwhile, up in Poland, another important rabbi was born in 1530: Moses Isserles. Unlike Karo, who was raised in the Sephardic-Jewish tradition, Isserles was an Ashkenazi Jew; I can't elaborate here, but there are a number of (relatively) minor differences in theology and custom between these two major sects of Judaism. In his mid-30s, Isserles became acquainted with Karo's work as soon as it was published in 1565. Concerned that Karo's book lacked the Ashkenazic perspective, Isserles began to write his own commentary and corrections to Karo, which came to be known as the *Mappah* or 'the tablecloth,' to accompany Karo's 'set table.'

So important was Isserles' commentary that, from 1578 onward, all editions of the *Shulchan Aruch* have included it, in the form of a sequence of '*Hagah*' (glosses) or remarks that follow each entry by Karo. Thus today, the joint work by Karo and Isserles is what has come to be known as "the" *Shulchan Aruch.*

Over the centuries, the *Shulchan Aruch*, rooted in Talmudic ideas, has come to be the dominant practical guide to Judaism around the world. It has been called "the most widely accepted compilation of Jewish law ever written" and a document "accepted by all of Jewry." Despite being a 'condensation of a condensation,' it is still extensive, running between 10 and 17 volumes, depending on format and translation. (It was this still-considerable length that caused another rabbi, Shlomo Ganzfried, to publish an even shorter version—the *Kitzur Shulchan Aruch*—in 1864. This one runs to a mere five volumes!). Again, we need to keep in mind that the *Shulchan Aruch* represents far more than just the thinking of the two men, Karo and Isserles; the work includes the comments, ideas, and opinions of hundreds of rabbis over literally two thousand years. It is a true distillation of Jewish thinking on a huge variety of practical, day-to-day matters. It is the essence of Judaism.

The *Shulchan Aruch* is organized in four main parts:

1) *Orach Chayim* ('way of life')
2) *Yoreh De'ah* ('understanding')
3) *Choshen Mishpat* ('shield of judgment')
4) *Even Ha'ezer* ('the stone of aid')

All are written in the form of 'laws' of what a Jew may or must do, or not do, with respect to a whole range of daily matters: prayer, the Sabbath, holidays, finances, marriage, mourning, diet, and the like. For someone who is non-Jewish, these laws often seem strange, bizarre, silly, contorted, or downright outrageous. And yet they are, nonetheless, the "law of the land" for Jews everywhere.

Of special interest here—and especially to Bischoff—are the laws that refer to the non-Jews (or Gentiles, or 'goyim'). Given that Jews were, and are, a small minority in every place that they inhabit (save Israel), these laws are of particular interest to both parties. Jews cannot avoid interacting with Gentiles, even if most Gentiles spend much or all of their lives never meeting a Jew in person. And yet, even those Gentiles who never personally interact with Jews are still affected by Jewish thinking and Jewish action on a daily basis. Gentiles living in the US, Canada, Europe, or Australia are directly affected, given that the governments in all these lands are heavily dominated by Jewish lobbies and Jewish financing. Gentiles who trade with these nations—people in China, Japan, Taiwan, Korea, India, and so on—are affected by Jewish trade policies and values. And Gentiles who are deemed 'enemies of Israel' (Palestine, Afghanistan, Iran, Iraq, Syria, Russia) continually feel the brunt of Jewish enmity via American financial and military might. Thus, one could say that virtually the entire planet is affected by Jewish thought and action; in this sense, all of humanity needs to understand Jewish attitudes toward Gentiles. Only in this way can the Gentiles of the world devise appropriate responses.

The Present Edition

Bischoff's book was originally published in 1929—a time when Germany was still struggling to recover from a loss in World War One and also attempting to deal with a heavily-Jewish Weimar government that seemed more interested in promoting Jewish interests than in restoring the German nation. Hitler's National Socialist party was gaining strength, emerging from its Bavarian origins to become a major national party. *Mein Kampf* had been in circulation for over three years, with its fundamental critique of Jewry, and other anti-Semitic publications (such as the Nuremberg-based weekly *Der Stürmer*) were steadily increasing circulation. Critics of the Jews routinely used lines from the Talmud to justify their views, but these were often ripped out of context or poorly translated, and in some cases simply wrong. Jewish groups were busy, as always, suing their critics for defamation, but lawyers and judges were in little position to determine the pros and cons of the arguments. All these considerations led Bischoff to publish his book.

Unfortunately, the editing of the original book leaves much to be desired. Apart from the usual German tendency toward long, rambling sentences and long, rambling paragraphs, the structure of the book is very complex and confusing. There are section numbers (letters, numbers, and Roman numerals), "main parts," two appendices (with multiple parts) containing, separately, textual notes and (often lengthy) endnotes. All in all: scholarly, but not reader-friendly. Here, I have attempted to untangle the many parts, trim out the irrelevant tangents, and tighten up the text. Notes and endnotes are now either integrated into the text itself or included as footnotes on the relevant page. (Most footnotes are Bischoff's, but some—marked as "Ed.:"—are my own, added for elaboration or clarification.) Portions of the appendix on the Talmud have been deleted because they had no apparent relevance to the topic of the book. And Bischoff's large "Fifth Main Part," with all the interesting passages from the *Shulchan Aruch*, has been divided into three units, one for each of the three areas Orach Chayim, Yoreh De'ah, and Choshen Mishpat (the fourth, Even Ha'ezer, was not addressed by Bischoff). In the end, my goal was to remove extraneous material and ensure that the central passages were clear and lucid.

After its initial publication in 1929, Bischoff released a second edition of his book in 1936, the year he died. Due to strong demand—in part, thanks to the resurgent National Socialist government—the publisher issued a 3rd edition in 1941 and then a final, 4th edition in 1942. It is from this last edition that I have taken the present translation.

As Bischoff himself admits, the first few parts of the book are somewhat "dry": preliminary material on history, structure, and contents of the *Shulchan Aruch*, along with summaries of current editions and recent critiques of it (through 1929). Not that this is unimportant; Bischoff includes many important and insightful remarks along the way, and the reader is strongly recommended to read through the full text. But the "meat" comes in the (now) last three chapters, which contain extended passages directly from the *Shulchan Aruch* along with Bischoff's commentary, as appropriate. For most readers, these will comprise the most interesting portions of the book. But not to be missed is the appendix, with some—quite literally—shocking statements taken directly from the Talmud regarding child sexuality. Suffice it to say here that Jews accept as permissible and moral things that most non-Jews would consider reprehensible and criminal.

Relevance for Today

All this raises the question of how relevant this is, in today's world in the 21st century. The answer is: extremely relevant.

If I may summarize the primary lessons to be learned from the following, it is that Jews—in the past and today—view themselves as separate, different, and more special than the rest of humanity. They are, in their view, the "chosen of God," and God has given to them alone his laws. God is *their* God, the Jewish God, the God of the Jews—and no one else. Since their laws come from God, they obviously trump any manmade civil laws of the sort that ordinary people live by, and that form the basis of civilized societies. Jews will try to follow civil law, but only when it is convenient and only when it is not superseded by any Jewish law.

All other people, the Gentiles, are non-believers and thus are heretics, infidels, the "godless." They have crosses in their churches and thus are "idolators." They foolishly follow civils laws instead of the laws in the Talmud and the *Shulchan Aruch.* Gentiles are unworthy of respect; and in some opinions, they are scarcely human at all—little better than animals. Just as one may own, use, abuse, and kill animals (for food, fur, etc.), so too many Jews believe that they can—and indeed, *should*—use, abuse, and yes, even kill Gentiles if it serves Jewish purposes. After all, look what it says *in the Bible itself*:

- Isaac says to his son Jacob, "Let peoples serve you, and nations bow down to you" (Gen 27:29);
- Moses tells his fellow Israelites, "you shall rule over many nations… [T]hey shall be afraid of you" (Deut 15:6);

- In Deuteronomy, God promises Jews "houses full of all good things, which [they] did not fill, and cisterns hewn out, which [they] did not hew, and vineyards and olive trees, which [they] did not plant" (6:11);
- We read in Isaiah, "foreigners shall build up your walls, and the kings shall minister to you…that men may bring you the wealth of nations" (60:10-11);
- And, ominously, "you [Jews] shall eat the wealth of nations" (61:6).

But what about all those passages that implore one to be kind to your "neighbor" and to aid your "brother"? Sadly for the Gentiles of the world, the "neighbor" and the "brother" only apply to the Jews—the Jewish neighbor, the Jewish brother. As we will see, Gentiles are explicitly excluded from the more benign sentiments of the OT. Time after time, Jews are encouraged to exploit, trick, deceive, or otherwise take advantage of non-Jews whenever they can get away with it.

Also distressing in the present day, with so many suffering from financial hardship, is the Jewish proclivity for cheating, exploiting, and even stealing from Gentiles for financial gain. Jews can charge non-Jews exploitive rates of interest; they can profit from Gentile errors; they need not repay loans; and they are not even compelled, in many cases, to pay taxes. Even in courts of law, Jews are "permitted" to lie, mislead, and deceive if it leads to them winning. As a general rule, Jews go by civil law *if it benefits them*; but if not, *then they go by Jewish law*. It's rather like a child who goes first to one parent, and then the other, looking for "the best deal." In the end, the only true rule is: *Is it best for the Jews?*

At this point, the apologist for the Jews may say: "But those laws are hundreds of years old. Things change, people change, values change. Even if Jews believed those things long ago, surely they don't anymore." That would be true for civil laws, but that's not what we have here. Here, we are dealing with the *laws of God*, and those don't change—ever. It doesn't matter how archaic such things sound to us, Jews don't care; they have an 'eternal law' and they have no intention of changing it. Hence, there is no progression, no evolution, no modernization in Jewish thinking. Their law is etched stone and it won't change.

Another apologist might raise a different issue: "All this only applies to strictly religious Jews, orthodox Jews; reform Jews and secular Jews don't hold to the Talmud or the *Shulchan Aruch*, and thus do not adhere to such moral obscenities." It's true that many Jews are non-orthodox, but it's *not* true that they do not adhere to those policies. As Bischoff explains, the *Shulchan Aruch* represents the ethos of all Jews everywhere, religious or otherwise. It embodies the essence of what it means to be a Jew. The whole mindset, the value system, and the worldview here are built into the Jewish psyche—pounded in, as it were, over thousands of years. A secular Jew can no more avoid Jewish arrogance and Jewish supremacy than he can stop breathing. Some are better at hiding it than others, but the same attitudes seem to be there, deep down, in all Jews. And when push comes to shove, these attitudes show their ugly face.

Yes, Jews are individuals. Yes, Jews disagree among themselves about many things. Yes, Jews range from conservative to liberal, from capitalist to communist to anarchist. But all these disagreements are disputes about tactics, not strategy. The strategy for all Jews is the same: Is it good for the Jew? The liberal tactic is not the same as the conservative tactic, and the Marxist tactic is not the same as the capitalist tactic. But the end goal is the same: increases in Jewish wealth and power, no matter the cost to others.

Before Bischoff, many people had recognized these malicious tendencies, but they lacked the knowledge—of the Hebrew language, of the massive Talmud, and of the less-massive *Shulchan Aruch*—to justify such things. In the present day, more and more people are recognizing troubling "patterns" among wealthy and prominent Jews: as financial swindlers, as con-artists, as liars, as parasites, as sexual predators, as dealers in pornography and drugs, as promoters of the basest and vilest 'popular culture.' These patterns are not figments of someone's imagination. They are very real, and are based in millennia-old Jewish precepts documented in, among other places, the *Shulchan Aruch*.

Now, after Bischoff's work—which resonates even more today than it did 90 years ago—people may begin to appreciate the "challenge" of the modern-day Jewish Question: What should we do about these Jews? Their deeply-embedded misanthropy, combined with their evident wealth and power, make for an extremely serious social problem—

arguably the greatest problem faced by humanity today. We can be grateful that Erich Bischoff chose to compile this text; it may yet serve a greater purpose than he could ever have imagined.

*****

Wherever possible, I have attempted to verify the passages cited by Bischoff, to correct any errors, and to adjust and clarify the English translations as appropriate. The reader is encouraged to verify these passages himself, rather than simply taking Bischoff's word for it. Today, with the Internet, there are on-line versions of both the Talmud and the *Shulchan Aruch*, though not all is in English. The website www.sefaria.org contains a useful English translation of many passages, as does www.en.wikisource.org. A simple web search of a given passage (for example, "Choshen Mishpat 156") will usually find useful text.

But there is also much obfuscation and confusing material on the Internet, so caution is advised. As a few minutes of searching will show, little is clear about these Jewish laws. It is almost as if…someone would rather have us not know the truth. But now, with the aid of Erich Bischoff and his excellent book, the path has become a little bit clearer for all.

THE BOOK OF THE SHULCHAN ARUCH

INTRODUCTION

ERICH BISCHOFF

"The Truth will set you free."
Gospel of John (8:32)

Never before has a book been written on the *Shulchan Aruch* that is intelligible for the non-professional and at the same time not written from the viewpoint of a biased party. I have attempted it, and hope that I have succeeded as well as with my books *Kabbalah* and the two volumes, *Elements of Kabbalah*, or like my best book, *Babylonian Astrology in the Midrash of the Talmud*. These works have introduced, for the first time, a field that has been more discussed than understood. If the present book similarly finds unanimous approval with Gentile and Jewish reviewers and readers, like the writings mentioned, and even my *Jesus and the Rabbis*, I would be pleased.

Yet this is hardly to be expected, given that the topic, the *Shulchan Aruch* itself, has always experienced the most varied appraisals. Theology professor D. Gustav Dalman writes so dispassionately and with such scientific discernment:

> It was…unlucky for the Jewish people, that the *Shulchan Aruch*, a book that represents Rabbinism in its harshest form, has attained such far-reaching validity. The strict distinction it makes between moral duties towards fellow compatriots and towards strangers could only have a confusing effect on the moral concepts of those who obey it. (*Jewish Foreign Law*, 1886, p. 39)

In contrast, the equally learned Dr. D. Hoffmann, an Orthodox Jewish lecturer at the Berlin Rabbinical Seminary, states

> that without exception, all suspicions and insults that have been directed against the *Shulchan Aruch* are generated

> from hatred and maliciousness, nurtured and reared in calumny, and have been accepted and disseminated through error and ignorance. Not the slightest stain remains on the character of our Rabbis, when this character is seen in the clear light of truth. (*The Shulchan Aruch*, 2nd ed., 1894, p 180ff)

Other circles have heard of the *Shulchan Aruch* perhaps first through *The Jewish Mirror* (*Der Judenspiegel*) of "Dr. Justus" (aka Ahron Briman), published in 1883, and through the newspaper articles and polemics that followed it. "Justus" took the "100 laws" of his *Jewish Mirror*, admittedly often in a highly distorted form, from the Jewish religious codex *Shulchan Aruch.*

However, the *Jewish Mirror* by itself would not have had such a strong impact, nor would the corresponding appraisal by Catholic professor Dr. Jacob Ecker have gone through such a high number of editions, if—as is still the case today for many genuinely or supposedly anti-Semitic writings—the Jews had not involuntarily advertised it in the form of a criminal complaint to the public prosecutor's office. The practice related to this was then still in its infancy. The criminal complaint and the official accusation were not directed against the publisher, Bonifacius Printing, but rather against the editor (Hoffmann) of the *Westphalian Merkur*, which featured some short excerpts from *The Jewish Mirror*, and it has not yet succeeded because of §166 but rather because of §130 of the Criminal Code, which was also much more reasonable. The trial of 10 December 1883 ended with the acquittal of the accused, which is becoming increasingly rare today under §166. A certain similarity persists today, in that a very unsuitable Jewish specialist, the local seminary teacher Treu, was invited as an expert and made all sorts of preposterous assertions.

Such trials of the religious press rarely serve objective truth, especially with lawsuits about the Talmud and the *Shulchan Aruch*, etc., because in these cases, neither the judges nor the public prosecutor understand what it is actually about. The trials often reveal the strangest views about these writings and what is connected to them, since the men involved do not have the least attachment to their content, nature, and current validity. They have never even seen such a work from the outside—further, the ability to translate a few sentences would not help to gain an insight into books printed in modern Hebrew or Aramaic, since laymen understand neither the context nor the meaning. More than a generation ago, when Pastor Thümmel, in a sharp polemic, accused Catholics of worshipping a "baked God," only German was spoken then, and the entire court was clear how this was to be judged under the criminal law. In the case of a Talmud or *Shulchan Aruch* passage, which the accused interprets in a completely different way than the complainants, the judges fail thoroughly, and naturally have no capacity to make judgements. And the public prosecutor's office, which is often sent dubious flyers, brochures, etc., as well as legal explanations by the complainant, is one-sidedly informed and, even with the best will of integrity, cannot assess the correctness of this "information."

Incidentally, even the crudest attacks on the teachings of the Talmud or the *Shulchan Aruch* cannot be dealt with in accordance with §166 of the Criminal Code, especially since these and similar writings, are only considered by the majority of German Jews to be sources of religious law, not "law books."

Due to its own natural lack of expertise, the court, to its embarrassment, has to rely on consultants (experts). Usually the public prosecutor—often at the suggestion of the person filing the complaint—suggests Jewish experts or those known to be pro-Jewish, while the accused suggests non-Jewish—sometimes anti-Semitic—experts; people then often try to reject those named by the other side. I do not want to go into this often very unpleasant matter, nor the natural bias of many experts and the lack of personal knowledge by most, including the average rabbi (whom the court often considers a priori to be an expert), Jewish preachers with a mere seminary background, etc., as well as the majority of non-Jewish experts. But I want to point out that the court is often as astute as mentioned before in view of opinions that are often completely contradictory, so that—to put it mildly—the possibility of a miscarriage of justice does not seem to be excluded by any means, just like the appeals and revisions in these trials prove this impression on one or the other litigant. No court is suitable for determining the objective truth about such complex disputes, only scholarship alone. Scripture serves my writing accordingly: "Everyone says what to him seems to be the truth, and the truth itself is commanded by God." Luckily, I have no reason to veer to the right or the left, or to vie for favor, but only to think and act like Martin Luther: "A good conscience, which is sure of the matter, does not dawdle and trifle, but tells the truth straight out, as it is in itself."

May this book be a teacher and advisor to many!

*****

I have divided the extensive materials as follows:

Part One gives, for the first time, a generally understandable, detailed, and impartial history of the development of the *Shulchan Aruch.*

Part Two offers a concise overview of the contents of the *Shulchan Aruch.*

Part Three attempts a short characterization of the *Shulchan Aruch* and its contemporary meaning.

Parts Four, Five, and Six contain translations of longer sections from the *Shulchan Aruch*, as well as shorter sections that are important for comprehension, and which have frequently been discussed incorrectly in polemics, with proofs from Talmudic sources.

The book includes two important appendices. Appendix A provides a number of translations from the Talmud, partly from sections that are used for comparison with the *Shulchan Aruch.* Appendix B critically examines, for the first time, the translations and editing of the *Shulchan Aruch* through 1929.

I could not spare the reader who wishes to dive deeply into the material the rather dry first three parts. I hope the sections that follow, with their livelier content, will reward him all the more for his patience.

The last three parts of this book, in which the *Shulchan Aruch* itself speaks to the reader, will be, for many, the most interesting part. But whoever wants to gain an accurate judgment about this peculiar work itself must not avoid the explanations of the first three parts. The path of oracles has always led through difficult terrain. The translations and explanations originate naturally from myself.

*****

The *Shulchan Aruch* (literally, the "Set Table") of Rabbi Joseph Karo (1488-1578), a contemporary of Martin Luther, is intended to be a concise manual of practical, authorized Jewish religious laws. In connection with his commentaries, this work indeed prevails unconditionally as such today among Eastern Jews, and with certain restrictions, among Orthodox Western Jews.

Karo himself stated the purpose of his work in the preface, "so the Rabbi will be clear on every practical law that he is asked about...and also so the young students learn it by heart, so, from a young age, they can become familiar with the practical laws."

The *Shulchan Aruch* is not a new, independent code of laws; rather, it forms in fact a certain keystone in the determination of the authorized, practical religious law that touches all areas of Jewish life, in a short form.

The *Shulchan Aruch* presupposes the Talmud, along with its attachments, in advance, just as a pocket atlas assumes the entirety of the corresponding cartographic survey sheets. The Talmud, on the other hand, presupposes the Old Testament together with the associated religious and legal tradition, just as a map series requires the physical and political configuration of the Earth's surface. In doing so, the maps, ordinance survey maps, and pocket atlases often distort nature just as much as the Talmud and *Shulchan Aruch* distort the Old Testament—especially a pocket atlas from 1564!

In order to understand the nature of the *Shulchan Aruch,* a brief overview of the development of Old Testament Talmudic religious law will therefore be useful. Following this we will become acquainted with the religious law books of Judaism that immediately precede the *Shulchan Aruch.* Next, we will briefly consider the emergence and completion of the *Shulchan Aruch,* and finally, the further development of religious law in Judaism up to the present.

— 1 —
On the History of the Shulchan Aruch

A. Old Testament-Rabbinical Religious Law

§1. The Judaism of the Talmud holds that Moses received a double "law"—the "Torah," i.e. the teachings, the religious law—on Mount Sinai: a *written* one and a *spoken* one. The former law Moses himself had, allegedly, written down in the five books of the Torah in the narrower sense, that is, the so-called Pentateuch: Genesis, Exodus, Leviticus, Numbers, and Deuteronomy. The "oral law," however, was passed on to Joshua only by word of mouth; likewise it was passed on to the elders of the community, from whom this "oral law" came down to the Talmudists via the prophets and the "menfolk of the great synagogue," and thus through to all the many generations.[1] A certain kernel of truth lies in this peculiar point of view.[2]

---

[1] Talmud *Avot* I, 1.

[2] The Old Testament itself acknowledges that the written law given to Moses "from Sinai" left many unanswered questions. Because "it was not clearly stated what one should do" with one who gathered wood on the Sabbath, or with another one who cursed God (Numbers 15:34; Leviticus 24:12), Moses had to consult God (or probably the 70 elders endowed by God with a kind of official spirit, Numbers 11:16f.). The decisions obtained are the first (and only reported in the Old Testament) oral statutes (*Halachôth*) that supplement the "Torah" (the written law). Furthermore, if the written law prohibited any "work" on the Sabbath, so a doctrinal tradition of what was to be regarded as such "work" at once had become necessary. Likewise, the rather incomplete provisions of the written law on matrimonial, civil and criminal law required more detailed (and over time more and more precise, and thus, in truth, expanded) provisions for their application to practical life; this was especially necessary with regard to whole areas of law, which the written law did not consider at all, e.g., commercial transactions, wills and guardianship, luxury, infanticide, and so on. Here a supplemental legal tradition necessarily had to be formed next to the written law.

Old Testament religious law, which can be found in the five books of Moses along with the stories, etc. from the time of the fathers, contains, according to the Jewish count, 613 Mitzvah or Regulations (namely, 248 commandments and 365 prohibitions). These form an "eternal law" and cannot be multiplied or reduced[3] once the Pentateuch was finally completed in Ezra's time (around 450 BC). Old laws tend to be the distillation of long-established legal practices and other customs. Such hallowed customs, sanctified through age and common observance, abound far more than the written law admits; for example, the peculiar Jewish rite of slaughter (the killing of the animals for sacrifice by opening the carotid artery, etc.) probably already existed before or during the time of Ezra, without the Pentateuch mentioning it or giving any instruction about it.

Secondly, the development of more than 500 years of Jewish life between the time of Ezra and the destruction of Jerusalem (from 450 BC to 70 AD) naturally created a considerable number of new customs and norms; in short, a religious-legal body of customs and practice, that was transmitted unwritten through tradition, and just as naturally, was still not found in the written law of the Pentateuch—or at the very most, a rudimentary recognition here and there.

All of the material handed down, which had gained religious-legal validity alongside and after the written law, was attributed to God's spoken message (alongside the written one) to Moses, and named them, in order to signify their real or reputedly venerable age, "*Halachôth le-Moscheh mi-Sinai*" ("Statutes of Moses from Sinai"), i.e. statutes given orally to Moses on Sinai. According to the Rabbinical view, these include, for example, the above-mentioned slaughter ritual, the regulations on the preparation of the roll-shaped Pentateuch texts (Torah scrolls) and the phylacteries (Thephillin). They also include the statutes (in truth only Rabbinical ones) about the 39 forbidden forms of work on the Sabbath, and even the strange statute that a girl, violated before the end of the third year of life, could be married later to a man of priestly lineage (who was normally only allowed to marry a virgin).[4] Later, the view of this oral transmission by God to Moses was even exaggerated to such an extent

---

[3] Deuteronomy 4:2 and Talmud *Temurah* 16a.
[4] Talmud *Niddah* 45a; see appendix.

that supposedly the entire Talmud, and even everything that Rabbis would teach in the future, had been revealed to Moses on Sinai.[5]

§2. In addition, the scribes (*Sophrim*), whose activities as interpreters of the scriptures had already developed in the Babylonian exile before Ezra, and in Palestine since Ezra, tried to interpret the customs and the religious-legal norms that arose after Moses from the text of the Pentateuch, no matter how much force was required. This interpretation, called the Midrash (*halachic*, i.e. religious-legal), is the order of the day in the Talmud, and is done with the greatest boldness, according to Goethe's well-known words: "Be fresh and cheerful when interpreting; if you don't lay it out, lay something underneath."

For example, in the Talmud Tractate *Hullin*, the above-mentioned rules about ritual butchering (slaughter) are sought from the Old Testament—where they are not to be found—in such a way that they are torturously derived from the words (Deuteronomy 12:21): "Slaughter your cattle and your sheep, as I commanded you." According to the Jewish view, this is supposed to point to a slaughter ritual that God orally communicated to Moses, while in truth it simply refers back to Deuteronomy 12:15: "You may slaughter and eat meat within all your gates" (but the burnt offering, only on the burnt offering altar)!

Furthermore, the principal post-Mosaic custom and (Rabbinical) regulation, to have three meals on the Sabbath day, is squeezed out of the three occurrences of the word "today" in the verse from Exodus 16:25: "Eat it (the manna) today, for the sabbath is today to the Lord, today you will not find it in the field." The Talmud Tractate *Hagigah* (Mishnah I 8) states very honestly about this interpretation: "The (first Rabbinical) dissolution of vows is floating in the air and has no scriptural basis." The statutes on the 39 rabbinically-forbidden works on the Sabbath, on the celebration of the feast (*Hagigah*) and on the neglecting of the sacred (*Mëilah*) are the mountains, hanging by a thread: scant scriptural grounding and many statutes derived from it. The scribes tried to validate their interpretation of the Scriptures and the religious-legal results obtained from them by working with the other scribes in the presence of their students in the "teaching houses"—usually in the evenings (because most

[5] *Niddah* 45a, *Berakhot* 5a, *Pe'ah* II 6.

were craftsmen, etc.)—set up for the purpose of discussion. By a majority decision or the consent of particularly respected authorities among the scribes, a specific view, teaching, etc. was then raised to the "*Halachah*", i.e. to a normative statute, and transmitted initially by way of mouth.

§3. The Mishnah, the basis of the Talmud, is the authoritative collection of the validated *Halachoth*, written by the "Patriarch" Rabbi Jehudah I, who last lived in Sepphoris (in Palestine), the grandson of Gamaliel I, towards the end of the 2nd century AD. It does not produce the "*Halachoth*" (in so-called "Midrasch"-form) in connection to the individual chapters of the Pentateuch according to their order, although the "*Halachoth*" arises from an interpretation of the Pentateuch (see above), but rather it distributes the material as a certain system[6] in six orders ('Sedarim';

---

[6] No Semitic Code of Law, no oriental writings at all, knows real systematics in the general assessment as well as in the inner structure of the material. Whereas Western thinking, especially since Aristotle, derives the particular thoughts and cases strictly logically from the general main thoughts and main cases, subordinates the particular to the general in all parts and thus erects a strictly articulated structure of thought, going, as it were, vertically from top to bottom, the Oriental builds the individual case, as the opportunity arises, by means of, so to speak, the horizontal connection of thoughts (the association of ideas), carelessly side by side, rather unconcerned about various contradictions and logical deficiencies. So this is the case with the Assyrian-Babylonian laws, with those scattered in the Koran, and also in the "Books of Moses". Already, the main and original law, the Ten Commandments, appears in Exodus 20:7ff. and Deuteronomy 5:7ff., in two different versions, the remaining regulations are incoherent and appear in several, sometimes conflicting versions. "This Torah was a work written without a plan, full of repetitions and contradictions. Nowhere is a clear disposition to be seen. Sentences and chapters follow one another without any connection." (Jakob Fromer, *The Talmud*, 1920, p. 29.)

That the Mishnah at least makes an attempt to arrange the religious-legal material contained in it according to a certain factual disposition, Fromer (p. 96) rightly attributes to the educating influence of Hellenistic (late Greek, thus, Occidental/Western) spirit on its arrangement. Just as appropriately, however, he calls this attempt unsuccessful and says correctly:

> "Even an overview of the titles of the six orders shows that this framework cannot contain the entire content. Talmudic tractates, like "Praises" (*Berakhot*), "Vows" (*Nedarim*), "The Sanctified" (*Nazir*), "Fathers" (*Avot*), and "The Unsanctified Slaughtering of Animals" (*Hullin*), do not fit anywhere. Therefore, they had to be inserted arbitrarily. Also the titles of the arrangement are not always

singular 'seder') and within these again to individual treatises, and their chapters and paragraphs.[7]

Accordingly, the reference to the underlying passages of the Old Testament is usually missing. As a rule, the individual doctrines are listed without naming their author; they are then called "Mishnah per se" and count as the undisputed norm or "*Halachah*". Sometimes, out of respect, the dissenting view of a respected Rabbi is given, but this is not usually counted as "*Halachah*," especially when it is followed by the majority view with the words "But the scholars say." At times, however, this majority view is extended or restricted by a great authority. Sometimes, short practical justifications of the simple doctrinal norms or explanatory cases from life are given.[8]

---

correct. ... The sequence of the Tractates lacks any logical principle. It is the worst with the sequence of the chapters and sections."

[7] The names of the 6 orders are: I. ***Zeraim*** ("seeds", rural taxes for the priests, etc.; preceded by the Tractate "*Berakhot*", (see above). II. ***Moed*** ("feast"; Sabbath, Passover, Day of Atonement, Feast of Tabernacles, New Year, fasting, half-holidays, pilgrimages, etc.) III. ***Nashim*** ("Women"; marriages in law, marriage contracts, divorce, adultery, wedlock; included are "*Nedarim*" and "*Nazir*", see above.). IV. ***Nezikin*** ("Damage"; civil and criminal law. Included is the marital collection "Sayings of the Fathers".) V. ***Kodashim*** ("Holy things"; sacrifices, grain offerings, etc. "*Hullin*" is included, see above). And VI. ***Tohorot*** ("Pure", i.e. defilements of containers, from a dead person, from leprosy, etc.; unclean fruits, cleansing ashes, immersion baths, washing hands, menstruation, gonorrhea, etc.). Each "order" contains a number (7-12) of shorter or (usually) longer "Tractates". See Appendix A for details.

[8] 1. Example of "Mishnah par excellence": (Talmud, *Bava Kamma* IV 3, Conclusion) "If the ox of a Jew hits the ox of a non-Jew, he is free (i.e. his owner does not have to pay compensation for the damage). But if the ox of a non-Jew hits the ox of a Jew, then he (that is, the owner) has to make good on all the damages (done) whether it (the ox of the non-Jew) had kicked or had been kicked. 2. Addition of the (non-normative) opinion of a respected scholar: *Berakhot* VI 8, Conclusion) "He who drinks water for his thirst, pronounces (on it) the blessing: 'Praised be He, through whose words everything came.' Rabbi Tarphon says: (He speaks.) 'Who created many souls and their hardships." 3. The majority of the scholars are the norm: (*Pe'ah* III 4) "If there are onion beds between the green cabbage, according to Rabbi Jose's opinion, the "Ackerwinkel" fee (the "corner of the field" donated to the poor) is to be paid for each individual bed. The scholars, however, say, "From one, for all." 4. Extension of this norm by a great scholar: (*Berakhot* I 1) "From when does one say the formula 'Hear Israel' in the evening? From the hour when the priests

§4. The Gemara (or the "Talmud" in the narrower sense) contains the disputations of the Palestinian and the Babylonian Rabbis about the Mishnah and the religious-legal (Halachic) materials handed down in the Palestinian "schools" (the teaching houses for scribes) from Tiberias, Caesarea, and Sepphoris and in the Babylonian "schools" from Nehardea, Sura, and Pumbeditha. Today, the Talmud is understood to mean (in a broader sense):

1. *The Palestinian Talmud* (also "the Jerusalem Talmud") = Mishnah and Palestinian Gemara;
2. *The Babylonian Talmud* = Mishnah and the Babylonian Gemara.

When one speaks of the "Talmud" per se, the Babylonian Talmud is meant. It is usually printed in twelve folio volumes with the same number of pages and pagination in each edition. It is quoted in such a way that refers to the name of the treatise, the leaf or page number, and their location on the front or reverse side of the page, eg. *Avodah Zarah* 2b = Talmud Treatise "Idolatry", page 2, reverse side. (In the case of the Palestinian Talmud, the chapter and paragraph of the Mishnah tract to which the Palestinian Germar belongs is usually quoted: pal. *Avodah Zarah* I 1.) The Palestinian Talmud was completed at the beginning of the 5th century AD, the Babylonian in the first half of the 6th century AD. The former is mostly written in Western Aramaic, the latter mostly in Eastern Aramaic. The Babylonian Talmud is considered authoritative.

The Gemara, or the Talmud in the narrower sense, completely lacks the systematic organization that can at least still be found, to some extent, in the Mishnah, even if only in the lax, Oriental sense. First, the Gemara by no means contains only the religious-legal discussions of the Rabbis from the 5th through the 6th century about what is to be regarded as a religious norm (*Hachalah*). It also consists to a large extent of the (non-normative) Haggadah, i.e. of expressions of opinion about all sorts of

---

go into the sanctuary to eat their offering, until the first vigil of the night; (this is) the teaching of Rabbi Eliezer. But the scholars say: until midnight. However, Rabban Gamaliel says: until the first ray of dawn rises."

things (Bible explanations, stories, ethics and its opposite, etc. etc) scattered throughout.[9]

After this, the "halachic" discussion continually digresses from the actual subject matter, brings in things that do not belong, and puts things that should belong together in distant places of the same tractate, or often even in a completely different tractate, where they are dropped in completely incoherently. "The digressions," says Fromer (*The Talmud*, p. 109) correctly, "are the rule in the Gemara. Everything is spoken of randomly and on a whim." In only a few places did the final editors of the Talmud (the "Saboraeans" of the 5th and 6th centuries A.D.) record what, in their day, was considered the norm of religious law (*Halachah*); in the Mishnah, this is the case only three times. In many cases, a Talmudic discussion comes to nothing or is expressly abandoned as inconclusive.

In order to find out from this jumble of disputing opinions what is to be regarded as a doctrinal norm (*Halachah*), various rules have later been established—which, however, are only conditionally valid. Such rules are, for example, collected in the *Séder Thannaïm wa-Amoraîm*. General principles for what is to be considered Halachah include: Agreement with a *Minhag* (custom) long since practiced, the origin of the teaching rising from a generally recognized authority, a generally-recognized scriptural proof for such a doctrine, and above all, finally, a majority decision or a majority statement in favor of it. But this is by no means necessarily true. If, for example, in such a majority decision the votes have not

[9] Compare my *Talmud Catechism*, 1904; also, for example, the bibliography in Strack, *Introduction to the Talmud and Midrash*, 5th Edition (1921), where writings based on the Talmud are given on the following subjects: on the understanding the Old Testament (and the narrative); faith, cult, sects, superstition; ethics; on the understanding of the New Testament; philosophy, mathematics, linguistics, pedagogy; jurisprudence; history; geography; natural science and medicine; archeology; community development, weddings, etc.; slaves, crafts and technology; farming and hunting; home and clothing; accounting; measures, coins and weights; fraternizing, bathing, kissing, etc. One may say without exaggeration that the Talmudic rabbis speak of the greatest and smallest, of the most sublime and most extraordinary, of everything possible and impossible and something more, beautiful and ugly, loving and hateful, virtuous and sinful, edifying and reprehensible, and that while in form and content we "divide the spirits," for the true Talmudist "the one as well as the other opinions are words of the living God" (*Gittin* 6b, *Hagigah* 3b).

been explicitly counted, or a generally recognized authority has spoken out against this decision, it is not considered *halachah* (a binding norm).

Furthermore, there are a significant number of such norms by which one was not allowed to act in spite of their public recognition. "Everyone could nevertheless … proceed according to the view he held; the practice was always a fluctuating one" (Tschernowitz, *The Development of the Shulchan-Aruch*, 1915, p. 14). From the "sea of the Talmud" one can fish a reason for almost every opinion (also in a religious-legal sense), just as it is said in the *Sophrim* Tractate (Chapter 16): "God gave Moses the religious law, in such a way that the same thing can be declared unclean in 49 ways and clean in 49 ways."

§5. The "Decisors", who sought to determine the Talmudic religious-legal norms (*Halachah*) from case to case in legal opinions, are the *Gaonen* i.e. the heads of the Talmudic schools in Babylonia, especially in Pumbeditha and Sura, who stood in the highest esteem of the Talmudic authorities from about 600 to 1038 AD. Since Talmudic studies no longer existed in the West, or did not exist yet, the foreign Jewish communities of various countries turned to them with all kinds of important questions of religious law and others matters. Their decisions ("Responses") were published to a large extent under the title "*Scheëlôth u-Theschubôth*" and form an important religious-legal source for the later Halachah collections ("Codices"). Even before the *Shulchan Aruch*, there were important codices of this kind, which had as their predecessors the Talmudic compendia.

Following the course of the discussion in the Talmud, the Talmud Compendia (or religious-legal excerpts from the Talmud), using the legal opinions of the Gaonens and other Rabbinic authorities, attempt to establish and collect the *halachah* (norm) that are important for religious-legal practice. Particularly noteworthy here are:

1. The Halachôth of Alfasi (Rabbi Isaac ben Jacob of Fez, 1013 to 1103 AD). This follows the views of Spanish Halachah research.

2. The Asheri of Rabbi Asher ben Jechiel (or Rosch, 1250 to 1327 AD). An excerpt from it: *Piské ha-Rosch*. This "Asheri" is included in most

major editions of the Babylonian Talmud. It follows French-German Halachah research.

3. The *Piské Thosaphôth* (14th century AD), religious-legal conclusions from the Talmud Explanations (*Thosaphoth*) of the German and French Rabbis of the 12th and 13th centuries. They are found in the Talmud editions behind the *Thosaphoth* (located in the outer margin of each page of the Talmud) of the individual Talmud tractates.

B. The "Codices" before the *Shulchan Aruch*

The "Codices" or religious law books of Judaism differ from the above-mentioned Talmudic compendia primarily in that they do not (like the latter) slavishly provide a connection to the confusing Talmudic discussions of the Gemara, but seek to group it in an independent arrangement.

§6. The Mishnèh Torah ("Repetition of the Law") of Moses ben Maimon—commonly known as Maimonides (1135 to 1204 AD), according to his 14 books, also called *Jad chasakah* ("Strong Hand"). This was written in good modern Hebrew around 1169, and is the first systematic exposition of Jewish religious law, revealing a trained Jewish-Arabic Aristotelian thinker, in the logical and clear manner of its presentation. He is quoted not according to his 14 books, but rather according to the titles of the individual sections and according to their chapters and paragraphs. Thus he is quoted: "Maimonides, *Jad chasakah* XXVI, *Hilchoth Sanhedrin* (Statutes on the Courts) 7," or more succinctly: "Maimonides *Hilchoth Sanhedrin* 7." Maimonides states that the purpose of his great work was "that the oral Torah (the Rabbinical religious law) be organized and accessible to everyone, and that it would no longer be necessary to consult any other work for information about any *Halachah* (religious-legal norm)".

Thus he intended to offer a conclusive, systematically-ordered Jewish religious-legal codex, a "second Torah." This was to complement the first one, the Old Testament—which he had treated explanatorily in his "Book of Commandments"—in a similar way that the Mishnah had attempted to do at the time. But Maimonides went far beyond the Mishnah by incorporating the *Halachoth* (religious-legal norms) developed by the authorities of the entire Talmud and the various religious law Midrash works, as well the *halachoth* (religious-legal norms) developed by the Gaonens.

In contrast to Alfasi and Rosch (see §5 above), Maimonides took into account not only the norms valid for the present, but also those which presuppose the existence of the temple services, the Jewish state, etc., so that his work would also be valid for the future (messianic) time when the temple, the sacrifices, Jewish kingship, and Jewish rule would be restored. On the other hand, due to living in Spain until age 13, in Fez until 30, and then permanently in Egypt, he was not sufficiently acquainted with the significant *Halachah* research and development in France and Germany. Thus it happened that, in addition to enthusiastic followers, sharp detractors criticized his methods as too philosophical, too arbitrary, and not caustic enough, repudiating his work, on the one hand, on the basis of excessive consideration of things obsolete, and on the other hand, on too little consideration of newer, alternative religious-legal Praxis.

Since the *Jad Chasakah* of Maimonides is to a large extent the spiritual father of the *Shulchan Aruch*—whose two producers, Karo and Isserles,[10] despite opposition to many individual details, were equally admirers of Maimonides—selected important passages from Maimonides are reproduced here in translation. The first one will serve as a lesson to the Jewish apologists who euphemistically interpret the phrase "for the sake of peace"—words frequently used by Maimonides and in the *Shulchan Aruch*—as "to create peace in the world" or even as "for the benefit of society," which is nonsense!

a) Maimonides, *Hilchôch abodah sarah* (Statutes of Idolatry) X 5ff.:

> "One gives food to the poor of the idolaters (non-Jews), and at the same time, to the Jewish poor, for the sake of peace; they are also not to be prevented from gleaning in the field, etc., for the sake of peace. One inquires after their well-being, even at one of their festivals, for the sake of

[10] Ed.: Rabbi Moses Isserles (1530-1572) was a Polish Ashkenazi Jew who wrote a significant number of notes to Karo's original text, and which became incorporated into the *Shulchan Aruch* itself. Thus, both men are, in a sense, the "authors" of the work. See section 10 below.

> peace. But one must never salute them repeatedly, nor enter the house of an idolater (non-Jew) on his holiday to greet him. If you meet him on the street, you may greet him softly and with a bowed head.
>
> However, all this only applies to the time when the Jews live in exile (outside Palestine) and are scattered among the peoples, or where the idolaters (non-Jews) have the upper hand over the Jews. But if the Jews have the upper hand over the idolaters (non-Jews), it is forbidden for us to tolerate any of them among us, even if they are only there accidentally and are temporarily checked in one place (by us), or they move trade from one place to another."

The *Shulchan Aruch* also says (*Yoreh De'ah* 151:12) that it is permissible to give alms to the non-Jewish poor, etc., "for the sake of peace." Marx-Dalman rightly remarks that, "for the sake of peace" has no other sense here than that used in the *Shulchan Aruch* by Karo and Isserles, as well as by Maimonides (*Hilchôth avodah zarah* IX 10), "*because of hatred*" (i.e. in order to avoid hatred). But this strange "love of peace" *ceases immediately as soon as one no longer needs it*, Maimonides admits in dry words—words that the apologists like to suppress! Marx-Dalman aptly says: "The motive for showing consideration for a peaceful understanding with the pagans is morally worthless as long as the consideration is regarded as only an emergency required by the present situation of the Jews." The translation, "for the sake of blessed peace", is factually quite correct; in the legal norms cited, this expression has no ethical, but a very practical meaning, just like the expression used in the *Shulchan Aruch* and elsewhere, that something is forbidden if "desecration of the (divine) Name" is to be feared; the simple meaning of the high-sounding expression is: if the matter is expected to be exposed, and thereby, Jewry (and its God with it) would come into bad repute.

The more tolerant views of modern Jewish authors should by no means be interpreted into the old legal sources. And so it also remains true that, for Maimonides, the Christians also belong to the "idolaters" in the passage quoted above, because he "considers them idolaters in every respect" (Marx-Dalman), while, for the *Shulchan Aruch*, they "are still only idolaters in a certain respect." If D. Hoffmann and others were correct in their view that, in Maimonides, the Christians took the position of "limited proselytes" to Judaism, they would have to concede that, according to Maimonides, *a Jew could then kill a Christian*; for Maimonides (*Hilchôth rozëach* II 1 1) established the principle as a religious-legal norm (Halachah): "A Jew who kills a limited proselyte, will not be killed by the (Jewish) court because of it"! But Maimonides is even more honest, and immediately adds: "And it need not be said that he will certainly not be killed for killing a non-Jew"! Are these also "Paths of Peace"?

b) A similarly "tolerant" attitude of Maimonides towards non-Jews is also shown in the passage of Maimonides, *Issuré biâh* (Statutes on the forbidden concourse) 4f.: "Know, the future (eternal) life belongs only to the righteous, and that is the Jews. … All (non-Jewish) peoples will be destroyed, but the Jews will endure."

c) Maimonides *Hilchôth aboda sarah* 18: "A Jewess should not nurse the son of an idolater,[11] because by so doing she would bring up a servant of idolatry; she should also not perform midwifery services for an idolatrous woman giving birth. But if she gets paid (!), she may do so, in order to prevent hostility".[12]

d) The Old Testament states that a convicted thief must compensate doubly the "neighbor" from whom he has stolen (Exodus 22:9). Maimonides, however, establishes as a religious-legal norm (*Hilchôth genëbâh* 1): "Whoever steals from an idolater only pays back the simple value of what was stolen; for it is said (Exodus 22:9): He must give back to his neighbor (i.e. the Jew) twice over, but not to an idolater."

e) According to the New Testament (Leviticus 5:20ff.), a Jew who has (falsely) denied a finding or a debt to his neighbor under oath and was subsequently convicted of the false oath must restore the value of the falsely-denied item, and add an additional one fifth to it. Maimonides, however, states as Halachah (*Hilchôfh gesëlâh* 7): "Whoever has sworn a

---

[11] Ed.: Note that every occurrence of the word 'idolator' simply means 'non-Jew.'

[12] Cf. Talmud *Avodah Zarah* 26a; *Shulchan Aruch*, Orach Chayim 330,2 (below).

(false) oath against an idolater (and has been convicted of it), pays back the simple value, but is not obligated (as with the Jew) to pay (also) the fifth part, because it says (Leviticus 5:20ff.): "If he denies anything to his neighbor!"

f) Maimonides, *Hilchôth gesëlâh* 11:

> "That which is lost by an idolater is permitted (to be kept); for it is said, 'With all that is lost by thy brother' (Deut. 22:3). Whoever gives it back commits a transgression, because by doing so he strengthens the power of the godless of the world (the non-Jews). But if he returns it to sanctify the Name (of God), so that the Jews may be praised and it may be known that they are honest people, it (the return) is to be praised." (Taken literally from the *Shulchan Aruch,* Choshen Mishpat 266,1—see below.)

The idolater—thus for Maimonides, also the Christian—is therefore *not* the Jew's neighbor, but a "godless person of the world" and has no claim on the Jewish finder for the return of the lost object. Jakob ben Ascher in his *Arbaah Turim,* Choshen Mishpat 266, regarding the prohibition against returning the lost to an idolater, intended this to mean only the real idol worshippers, but not other non-Jews (*goyim*). Joseph Karo accuses him of mild hypocrisy for this reason in his Tur commentary *Beit Yosef* on the Choshen Mishpat 266, saying:

> "According to the clear wording of the law (Deuteronomy 22:3), all non-Jews (goyim) are here equal, whether they be (real) idolaters or not; for they are not 'your brothers'. Our Rabbi (Jakob ben Ascher) was not precise when he named here only the (real) idolaters. Perhaps he did so because in the land of Edom (Christian Europe), the baptized Jews suspect the Jews because of this and similar laws by the king, to which the sages (of the Jews, appeasing apologetically) replied that this referred only to the goyim of Talmudic times, who had worshipped idols and had not proclaimed the Creator of the world; the goyim of the present

> time, who profess the Creator of the world, would not be counted among the idolaters, neither by this law nor by other similar ones."

According to Karo, this assertion by the "wise men" of the time is an apologetic ruse; Karo considers the misappropriation of findings from all non-Jews—thus also Christians—to be divinely permissible!

g) Maimonides, *Hilchôch avodah zarah* 1: "It is forbidden to have mercy on the idolaters; for it is said (Deut 7:2): 'You shall show them no mercy!'"

h) Maimonides *Hilchôth Shabbath* (Sabbath Laws) 20f.:

> "If there are Gentiles and Jews in a courtyard, even just one Jew and a thousand Gentiles, and a building collapses on them (on the Sabbath), so the rubble will be cleared away from all of them, because of the Jew. If one of them leaves and goes into another courtyard, where a ruin falls on him there, the rubble is also cleared away from him (despite the Sabbath); for perhaps the one who left is the Jew, and those who remained behind are the non-Jews.
>
> But if all have set out to go from one courtyard to the next, but at the time of their departure one of them has departed and gone to another courtyard, where a ruin has fallen on him, however, it is not known who he is, they do not clear away the rubble from him (on the Sabbath); because since they have all set out, there is no Jew (anymore in the first courtyard), and anyone who moves away from them during their procession is considered to belong to the (non-Jewish majority) and because of him the rubble is not removed on the Sabbath."

i) Maimonides, *Hilchôth ischûth* (Marriage Statutes) 3: "A (Jewish) man may take any number of wives, even a hundred, either at once or one after another, and his wife cannot prevent him, provided that he able to give each their proper clothing, food, and conjugal duty." Compare with the Arbaah Turim of Jacob ben Asher in *Even Ha'ezer* 1:

> "A Jew may take any number of wives ... provided that he can support them. The Sages (Scholars), however, offer the good advice that the man (the Jew) should not take more than *four* wives. Where the custom is to take only one wife, it is not permitted to take another wife while still with the one. Rabbi Gerson put a great ban on anyone who would add another one to his wife. However, this decree has not spread to all countries, and he imposed the ban only until the end of the 5th [Jewish] millennium."

That is, until 1240 AD. Theoretically, the ban on polygamy has also lost its force for Western Jews; practically, their legal polygamy is still prevented, at least temporarily, by the public prosecutor and the purse, in civilized Europe also by the ethical culture, and probably also by the prospect of multiple mothers-in-law.

j) Maimonides, *Hilchôth melachîm* (Royal Law) 3: "The non-Jew has no valid marriage." Likewise already a hundred years earlier, the Bible and Talmud interpreter Raschi: a) at Leviticus 20:10: "That he has broken the marriage with his neighbor's wife, excludes the wife of a Gentile; we learn from this that the non-Jew has no valid marriage;" b) at Sanhedrin 52b: "We hear from this that the non-Jew has no valid marriage."

k) Maimonides, *Hilchôth malweh we-loweh* (Law of Obligations) 1:

> "One borrows from a non-Jew and tenants and also lends to them usuriously (at interest); for it says (Deuteronomy 23:20): 'You shall not profiteer on your brother.' On your brother (the Jew) it is forbidden, on the rest of the world (the non-Jews) it is permitted."

The same Maimonides says more sharply in the *Sèpher mitzwôth* (Book of Commandments, regarding Deuteronomy 34:20).

> "The 198th precept is that God has commanded usury to be taken from the non-Jew, and that we can only then lend to him (when he agrees to it), so that we do not benefit him or render help, *but rather cause him harm*, even if we ourselves do not benefit from it".[13]

Despite all the denials of the apologists, the fact that what is meant is not harmless taking of interest, but *real usury*, is evident not only from Maimonides' saying "to cause harm", but also, for example, from Rashi on Exodus 22.19: "Usury is like the bite of a small snake, which makes a small wound on a man's foot, so that he does not notice it, but which soon causes a heated swelling up to the spine. Likewise, one does not (at first) feel usury until it increases and causes great loss of wealth."

§7. The Arbaä Turim (also called simply "Turim" or "the Tur") of Jacob ben Asher (c. 1280 - c. 1340) are named after Exodus 28:17 ("Four Rows"), and written around 1321. The author is often referred to as "Bàal ha-Turim" after his work. He carefully takes into account the further development of Halakhah in the hundred years that have passed since Maimonides' codex, but, in accordance with his practical purpose, he does not (as Maimonides does) offer the norms relating to temple services, etc., which are impracticable for modern religious practice. [...]

§8. The *Beit Yosef* ("House of Joseph," cf. Genesis 43:26) of Joseph Karo first gives for each passage of the "Turim", the Talmudic (or Midrash) source and the views of all Spanish, French, and German Jewish religious-legal authorities from the 200 years since the death of Rosch, which Karo collected over 20 years (1522-1542) from more than 32 cited works. To these he added the statutes on Levirate marriage, Hebe, grain tithes, idolatry, etc., although, for example, Levirate marriage had already almost or completely fallen into disuse in many countries. Thirdly, in a bold fashion, he undertook to establish forever, on his own initiative, what was *Halachah* (a valid religious-legal norm) in each case, in order

---

[13] Ed.: This is a remarkable admission: that Jews will actively harm Gentiles even when it is unaccompanied by immediate gain. It seems that Gentile harm, in itself, is valued by the Jews.

to counter the fragmentation of views that was all too evident from his sources and to bring about uniform religious-legal rulings.

Karo's approach is very simple, but also very mechanical: he takes into account only Alfasi, Maimonides, and Ascheri as the main representatives of the Spanish-Oriental and French religious law. If two of these authorities agree, he follows them. Since most of the time Alfasi and Maimonides agree as representatives of the first direction, Karo's decisions mostly favor the Spanish, or rather Spanish-Oriental, scholars.[14] And Western religious law was wrongly disregarded, which brought Karo some disapproval, for example, from Isserles (see below §10). For the elaboration of the *Beit Yosef*, Karo needed another 12 years (1542-54) beyond the 20 years of work gathering materials.

Only then—eight years after Luther's death in 1546—was the newest and hitherto largest work on Jewish religious law completed, consisting of the folios of *Beit Yosef!* But the immense work was much too extensive for the practical use that Karo wanted it to serve. The times demanded a practical, concise summary of the applicable religious law, a compendium of *Halachah*. Old demands emerged intensified. People wanted "abbreviated norms" (abbreviated *Halachah*)—some in order to devote themselves to the study of Kabbalah, others in order to be able to devote themselves to philosophy and some other modern secular science, at least on the side, and not to have to "waste their entire life with the study of the law."

Thus, at the beginning of his seventies, Karo himself decided to write a practical excerpt from his monumental work, the *Beit Yosef*, which was only to summarize briefly and clearly the norms of religious law that were valid in his opinion, without the ballast of source references, explanations, and discussions. It was finished around 1563; in 1565 the new work was first printed in Venice: it was called — the *Shulchan Aruch*.

---

[14] Karo often follows Maimonides word-for-word. Mordechai Jaffa, in the preface to his "*Lebûsch orach chàjjim*", says: "Karo adopted most of the statutes based on Maimonides' version, because that is how it is done in the East, Karo's sphere of activity." Much of the *Shulchan Aruch* is simply an excerpt from the Mishnah Torah of Maimonides.

C. The *Shulchan Aruch* from 1565 until 1929

§9. The original *Shulchan Aruch.*

As noted, *Shulchan Aruch* means "set table" (after Psalms 23:5; cf. Ezekiel 23:41; Proverbs 9:2). About its author, Joseph Karo, see the preceding section §8. The first printed edition appeared (in quarto) in Venice 1564-65, the second (in folio) in Venice 1567: both without examination by the papal book censors, who later, for example, made the expressions denoting the non-Jews (Gentile, goy, etc) instead meaningless *akûm* ('star worshippers'), so that it would seem that Christians, for example, were never meant.

In the division of the material, the *Shulchan Aruch* (like the *Beit Yosef*, see above) follows the Araäthe Turim, thus also containing the four divisions or books:

1) Orach Chayim,
2) Yoreh De'ah
3) Choshen Mishpat,
4) Even Ha'ezer.

Karo offers only the bare norms—considered by him to be the final Halachah—without explanations, dissenting views, and source references, mostly in the version given to him by the revered Maimonides, which in many cases strives to make the original (e.g. Aramaic) wording of the sources more concise and easy to understand.

Karo wanted to give a (relatively) short review of Jewish religious law, for which he referred in the preface to the *Shulchan Aruch* to his *Beit Yosef* (see above, §8) for more detailed explanations, sources, etc. According to the same preface, he wanted it to be repeated every month from beginning to end, and thus gradually memorized by the rabbis. If Karo's *Shulchan Aruch*, according to the author's own statement, follows the purpose "that a rabbi is clear about every practical law about which he is asked," thereby "the law of the Lord is completed and becomes familiar in the mouth of every Jew." Then this cannot be interpreted in any other way than that Karo wanted at least all ordinary cases of practical Jewish religious-legal life to be decided quickly according to his work, in which he believed himself to have established the final *Halachah* (religious-legal norm). Otherwise, one could not understand the criticism of his rivals and the extension of Isserles (see below §10), that Karo in his *Shulchan Aruch,* if all its words were divine commandments transmitted by Moses, then it would also make no sense if Isserles emphatically points out the necessity of their verification by the study of the source works. This indicates that according to Karo's intention, the *Shulchan Aruch* should be, and was, used as an independent source of religious legal decisions.

Karo's reputation as a Cabbalist, especially among the Jews of the East, implicated that his *Shulchan Aruch* was surrounded with a kind of divine aura. The legend spread that an angel had gone through the different questions of the *Halachah* with him daily, and had told him heavenly secrets and God's joy about the *Shulchan Aruch,* plus he had revealed two mistakes found by God in it, which Karo had corrected immediately. Thus, the *Shulchan Aruch* is even considered here as a *divine revelation* and as a book reviewed by God himself, which accordingly was treated as an independent source of revelation!

According to the announcements cited by Ch. Chernovitz (*Origin of the Shulchan Aruch,* p. 30), Karo's work was accepted "in Palestine, Egypt, Damascus, Mesopotamia, Persia, Turkey and farther west" as the norm of decision, and as a result of the approval of 200 rabbis, the dictum applied: "He who follows the decisions of our master (Karo), follows 200 rabbis."

In the "West," i.e. primarily in Poland, where rabbinical scholarship had reached a high level, and in Germany (especially Bohemia), the work of Karo was viewed much more critically. While some Sephardic Jews from Spain had already criticized some inaccuracies in the *Shulchan Aruch* and attributed them to Karo's weakness due to old age or to the negligence of his students involved in the work, the German-Polish rabbis also rightly criticized Karo for having almost completely ignored the teaching and living standards of the Jews of their countries, which were recognized in theory and practice, in the determination of the norms of religious law. Even if Karo, who wrote remotely from these countries, did not know many of those norms, the main reason for his mistake lay in his inadequate majority method, in the application of which Ascheri, who represented the German norms, almost always came up short, in comparison with the Spanish-Oriental norms of Alfasi and Maimonides.

This methodological error was already evident in Karo's *Beit Yosef.* That is why the criticism of the representatives of the German-Polish orientation already turned against the work of Karo. The most significant of these detractors is Rabbi Moses Isserles from Krakow, in his own Turim commentary, *Darké Moscheh* ("The Ways of Moses," cf. Psalm 103,7). This work is as fundamental to Isserles' Hagahôth, to be mentioned in the next section, as the *Beit Yosef* is to the *Shulchan Aruch* of Karo. Out of ignorance or a certain deliberateness, for a long time (indeed, until today) Isserles has been presented as a modest collector of gleanings on both of Karo's works. It is to the credit of Tschernowitz to have strongly emphasized the truth that Isserles is a sharp opponent of Karo's method and a strict critic of his conclusions, and consequently of his established norms. Rightly Tschernowitz says in the work already cited:

> "Isserles' relation to Karo is strictly critical. In sharp expressions he refutes his conclusions. Expressions such as, 'his remarks are not illuminating,' 'his remarks are to be rejected,' 'his remarks are lame,' 'here he has committed an error,' can be found very often. Mainly Isserles was trying to establish the authority of German (and Polish) customs and norms, which Karo had left out."

The results of his "*Darké Mosheh*" were inserted by Isserles in the form of critical annotations (Hagahôth) into the edition of the *Shulchan Aruch* which he had arranged, in such a way that he had them printed in small letters behind the individual paragraphs of Karo's work or in brackets within the paragraphs.

§10. The Hagahôth of Isserles

After Karo died in 1575, Isserles published his *Shulchan Aruch* for the first time in 1578 from his residence in Krakow with his own Hagahôth (critical "additions") in folio. His two editions, like Karo's first editions, were not yet modified by Papal censorship. However, the edition of the *Shulchan Aruch* that had been completed in Venice in 1594, together with Isserles' annotations, were, for the first time, revised by the censors, as was the case with all subsequent editions of the *Shulchan Aruch* in the various places of publication. From then on, Karo's work, inseparably united with Isserles' notes, formed the "*Shulchan Aruch*" in the usual sense.

Isserles modestly calls his critical remarks "the tablecloth" (*Mappah*) to Karo's "set table" (*Shulchan Aruch*) in the then-common imagery. Just as modestly, he introduces the norms of the German-French-Polish authorities, contradicting the findings of Karo and the deviating customs from their countries and his own findings, with the words: "But others say" or "with us (in Germany and Poland) the custom is different" and so on. But this deference must not deceive us about the fact that under the ostensibly simple drafting of annotations, a sharp critic and rectifier is hidden. Sternly, the severe rebuke against Karo's arrogance in his way of establishing the norms of religious law, breaks right through these courtesies.

Isserles' practice of publishing his critical corrections and additions together with Karo's *Shulchan Aruch* itself was tremendously shrewd. As an independent refutation of Karo's quickly-proliferating book, his Hagahôth would probably have died away ineffectively, shortly afterward, like the polemical writings of Salomon Lurja and Chajjim bar Bezaleel. However, by causing his Hagahôth to henceforth always be appended to Karo's *Shulchan Aruch*, and thereby to become an inseparable constituent of the *Shulchan Aruch* as a whole, Isserles, through the modest form of annotation, ensured that his objections, corrections, and additions attained the same authority as Karo's original work. If, despite this, most translators of the *Shulchan Aruch* reproduce only Karo's original text without the Hagahôth of Isserles (which is probably sometimes not pleasing to modern sensibilities), they consciously or unconsciously deceive the non-expert reader about the true facts. What "the *Shulchan Aruch*" says is always Karo + Isserles.

§11. Main Jewish Commentaries

1. *Beér ha-golah* ("Fountain of Exile," cf. Exodus 2:15; abbreviated: Bahag) by Moses Ribkes (Ribkas; in Vilna, beginning of the 17th century) was the first of all commentaries to be printed together with the *Shulchan*

Aruch (Amsterdam 1661 and 62) and contains the source references for all the laws of the *Shulchan Aruch* as well as brief, often corrected or supplementary explanations; it is found printed with most versions of the *Shulchan Aruch.*

2. *Turé sahâb* ("Golden Rows") by David (ben Samuel) Halevi (in Ostrog and Lublin, d. 1667). Likewise, a commentary on the *Shulchan Aruch*, most importantly on the explanations of Yoreh De'ah. The commentary on Orach Chayim bears a special title Magén David ("The Shield of David." cf. 2 Sam. 22:3). He regards the *Shulchan Aruch* as an inviolable authority, which he defends against critics by explaining in detail the meanings of the individual passages and seeking to resolve contradictions.

3. *Sèpher meïràth ënàjim* ("The Book of the Illumination of the Eyes," cf. Psalms 19:10; Sma or Ma) by Joshua Falk (Kohen) in Lviv (1550 to 1614). Was completed only for the Chosen Mishpat portion. For each paragraph, the source and justification are given, then Karo's and especially Isserles' text (according to the first manuscript) is corrected, explained in detail and the contradictions are attempted to be balanced, at the same time many newly established norms are added.

4. *Siphthé Kohen* ("Lips of the Priest," cf. Malachi 2:7; abbreviated: Schach) by Sabbathai Kohen (Zedek; abbreviated: Kaz) in Lublin (1622-63). Commentary on Chosen Mishpat (copious material, but unorganized) and on Yoreh De'ah (excellent commentary; rich references to sources, reconciliation of contradictions between Karo and Isserles, defense of the *Shulchan Aruch* against all opponents). "Kaz" and Halevi (above 2.) make the triumph of the *Shulchan Aruch* definitive.

5. *Magén Abraham* ("The Shield of Abraham," cf. Gen 15:1) by Abraham (Halevi) Gumbinner in Kalisz (d. 1682) commentary in part on the Orach Chayim.

6. *Chelkàth mechokék* ("The Ruler's share," cf. Deut 33:21) by Moses Lima in Vilnius (died 1673). Commentary on the Even Ha'ezer.

7. *Baér hétéb* ("Well explained," Deut 27:8). "Short excerpts from many other commentaries, mostly printed with smaller editions of the *Shulchan Aruch* to replace the larger commentaries" (Hoffmann, The *Shulchan Aruch*, 2nd ed., 1894, p. 38). The excerpts are not always reliable.

Tschernowitz writes, "Each age added new commentaries, which often gave rise to further commentaries. Almost all the literature of the last generations was confined to the field of the *Shulchan Aruch* and its commentaries. In our time, the number of these commentaries printed along with it has risen to 40."

Hoffman describes the actual *Shulchan Aruch* or "*Shulchan Aruch* in the broadest sense" (as today still the authoritative "religious law of law-abiding Jews"), "the *Shulchan Aruch*, with the authoritative additions, explanations, and corrections that follow the text." Since "no work has yet appeared" that has "united these universally valid religious laws in a single code," the Orthodox rabbi is in many cases dependent on the oral instruction (*shimmush*) of his teachers who inform him of the view valid for practice in the numerous differences of opinion."

The older opponents of the *Shulchan Aruch* like Salomon Lurja (1510-73), Chajjim Bezaleel (16th century), Mordechai Jaffa (d. 1612), Joel Sirkes, Meïr Lublin, and Samuel Edels do not struggle against the spirit of the *Shulchan Aruch*, but only criticize the methodological mistakes of Karo and Isserles in determining the religious-legal norms.

Modern Reform Judaism, on the other hand, has technically renounced the *Shulchan Aruch*, in the same way that modern Protestantism, for example, has renounced the Formula of Concord in the post-Reformation period, during which the *Shulchan Aruch* came into being. The Eastern Jews still hold absolutely on to the *Shulchan Aruch*.[15]

---

[15] But see below, chapter 4, for an extended discussion on this matter. Compare *Graetz, Geschichte der Israeliten* (History of the Israelites) Vol. IX, 2nd ed., 1877, p. 133: "(The *Shulchan Aruch*) *forms to this day, for German and Polish Jews, the religious norm, the official Judaism*."

— 2 —
THE CONTENTS OF THE *SHULCHAN ARUCH*

The *Shulchan Aruch* consists of four main parts:

1) Orach Chayim
2) Yoreh De'ah
3) Choshen Mishpat
4) Even Ha'ezer

(1) Orach Chayim

- 27 chapters with 697 paragraphs.
- The *Shulchan Aruch* is always quoted according to the paragraph and their possible subdivisions, e.g. "Orach Chayim §1" or "Yoreh De'ah 142,10".

1. **Religious responsibilities in the morning**. §§1-7: 1. Getting up; 2. Dressing; 3. Conduct in the toilet; 4. Washing the hands; 5. Devotion while saying Blessings (Praying); 6. Saying blessings after leaving the toilet; 7. Saying blessings after passing urine.
2. **The "Tassels" (*Tzitzit*), the prayer shawl (*Tallit*), etc.** §§8-24.
3. **The Phylacteries [prayer straps].** Tefillin; §§25-45.
4. **The Blessings.** Berakhot; §§46-88: 46-57. Blessings in the morning at home and in the Synagogue; 58-88. The Recitation of the Formula "Shema," i.e. "Hear Israel", Deut 6:4-10.
5. **Prayers and their time**. §§89-127.
6. **The priestly blessing on the feast days**. §§128-134.
7. **The reading of the Torah (Pentateuch) scroll**. §§135-149.
8. **Synagogues, construction, and furnishings**. §§150-156.
9. **Table customs at meals, etc**. §§157-201.

10. **Blessings over pleasures**. §§202-231.
11. **Afternoon and evening prayer and marital cohabitation**. §§232-241: 232-234. Mishnah prayers; 235-239. "Listening" formulae and Evening prayers; 240. Sexual intercourse; 241. Urination in a naked state before bed.
12. **Observance of the Sabbath**. §§242-365.
13. **(Prohibited) "Activities" on the Sabbath, etc**. §§366-395.
14. **The way of the Sabbath, etc.** §§396-407.
15. **The extent of way of the Sabbath, etc**. §§408-416.
16. **The celebration of the new moon**. §§417-428.
17. **The celebration of the Passover**. §§429-494.
18. **Holidays**. §§495-529.
19. **Semi-holidays (intermediate holidays).** §§530-548.
20. **The Ninth of Av** (Fast day commemorating the destruction of Jerusalem [the second temple]); §§549-561.
21. **Other days of fasting.** §§562-580.
22. **The New Year's feast**. §§581-602.
23. **The Day of Atonement**. §§603-624.
24. **The Feast of the Tabernacles**. §§625-644.
25. **The celebratory bouquet of feast, etc**. §§645-669.
26. **The Feast of Hanukkah**. (The Festival of Lights or Consecration). §§670-685.
27. **The Feast of Purim**. §§686-697.

(2) Yoreh De'ah

- 35 chapters with 403 paragraphs.

1. **Slaughter.** §§1-28.
2. **Defective animals.** §§29-62.
3. **Meat from live animals.** §62.
4. **Meat, that a Gentile has had**. §63.
5. **Fat**. §64.
6. **Prohibition against tension veins and blood**. §§65-68.
7. **Salting of meat**. §§69-78.
8. **Clean and unclean animals**. §§79-85.
9. **Eggs**. §86.

10. **Meat and milk**. §§87-99.
11. **Unlawful mixing of food and vessels**. §§100-111.
12. **Food prepared by Gentiles**. §§112-22.
13. **Wine from Gentiles**. §§123-138.
14. **"Idolatry".** §§139-158.
15. **Interest, loans, etc**. §§159-177.
16. **Forbidden imitation of Gentiles; sorcery, etc**. §§178-182: 178. Imitation, etc.; 179f. Sorcery; 181. Shearing off the "four corners," i.e. the "side curls" at the temples and the corners of the beards; 182. Prohibition of wearing the clothes of the opposite sex.
17. **Female impurity**. §§183-202: 183-197. Menstruation; 198-200. Purifying immersion; 201f. Bathing opportunities.
18. **Vows**. §§203-235.
19. **Oaths**. §§236-239.
20. **Instructions for reverence to parents**. §§240-241.
21. **Likewise for Rabbis**. §§242-246: 245f. Obligation to study Jewish law.
22. **Almsgiving**. §§247-259.
23. **Circumcision**. §§260-266.
24. **Circumcision of Slaves**. §267.
25. **Proselytes**. §§268f.
26. **Torah scrolls** (Manuscripts of the Law, i.e., Pentateuch). §§270-284.
27. **The Mezuzah** (The doorpost scroll). §§285-291.
28. **Bird's nests**. §§292-294: 292. Prohibition of catching away the mother bird, Deut 22:6 f.; Of the eating of new grain before the 16th Nisan, Lev 23:14; Of eating the fruit of a tree less than 3 years old.
29. **Prohibition of the mixing of seeds, etc.** §§295-304.
30. **Ransoming of the firstborn**. §305.
31. **The first-born of pure cattle, etc**. §§306-321.
32. **Gifts for the priests**. §§322-333: 322ff. Raising dough; 331ff. Raising and tithing.
33. **Minor and major bans**. §334.
34. **Visiting the sick, nursing the sick, treatment of the dying**. §§335-339.

35. **Treatment of the dead**. §§340-403: 340. Tearing of clothes; 341. Mourning of the dead before burial; 342 Mourning after burial.

(3) Choshen Mishpat

- 29 Chapters with 427 paragraphs.

1. **Judges and their courts** (Their powers). §§1-27.
2. **Witnesses**. §§28-38.
3. **Lending and borrowing** (The Law of Obligations). §§39-96.
4. **Debt collection** (In general). §§97-106.
5. **And the like with orphans, etc**. §§107-120: 117ff. mortgages.
6. **And the like with messengers or agents**. §§121-128.
7. **Security**. §§129-132.
8. **Possession of movable property**. §§133-139.
9. **Possession of immovable property**. §§140-152.
10. **Damage to neighbors.** §§153-156.
11. **Community property**. §§157-175: 157ff. Community property; 171 ff. Partition; 175. Boundary disputes.
12. **Company transactions**. §§167-181.
13. **Messengers and brokers**. §§182-188.
14. **Purchase and sale**. §§189-226.
15. **Overreaching, etc**. §§227-240.
16. **Donations**. §§241-249.
17. **Donations from the sick, etc**. §§250-258.
18. **Lost and found**. §§259-271.
19. **Charging and discharging**. §272.
20. **Property without master; Goods of proselytes**. §§273-275.
21. **Inheritance**. §§276-290: 283 Gentile inheritance.
22. **Custody of property**. §§291-330: 291ff. Gratuitous: 303ff. Paid custody; 307 ff. Rent; 320 ff. Lease.
23. **Contracts for work**. §§331-339.
24. **Lending of moveable property (livestock, etc)**. §§340-347.
25. **Theft**. §§348-358.
26. **Robbery**. §§359-377.

27. **Compensation for self-inflicted damage**. §§378-388: 388 Punishment of braggarts.
28. **Compensation of the owner of livestock, etc**. §§389-419.
29. **Bodily injury and defamation, etc**. §§420-427.

(4) Even Ha'ezer

- 5 Chapters with 178 paragraphs.

1. **The Commandment of procreation**. §§1-6: 1. The commandment; 2-4 Descent of spouses; 5f. Congenital and acquired inability to procreate.
2. **Impediments to marriage, etc**. §§7-25: 7-22. Separative and suspensive impediments; 23-25. Onanism, sodomy, coitus.
3. **Marriage**. §§26-118: 26-56. Betrothal, etc.; 57-67 Marriage; 66-118. The entire marriage law.
4. **Divorce**. §§119-155.
5. **Brother-in-law marriage**. §§156-178: 156-168. Refusal (*Miûn*); 169 Renunciation of widowhood (*Chalizah*); 170-178. Appendix on fornication, lechery, adultery.

Some individual paragraphs contain very many subdivisions (numbers); e.g. Orach Chayim §128 contains 42, Yoreh De'ah §267 contains 81; other paragraphs in turn contain only one number, comprising a few lines.

The Additions of Isserles (see above, §10) are either in smaller print after the individual numbers to which they refer, or in the middle of them, with the same letters, only enclosed in brackets.

— 3 —
EVALUATING THE *SHULCHAN ARUCH*

A. The *Shulchan Aruch* is not an independent work. Its author Joseph Karo based the work on the "Codices", especially on the Mishnah Torah of Maimonides, which he often writes out literally; but the "Codices" go back to the Talmud compendia and to the Decisors in the Talmud. There should be scarcely anything in Karos' *Shulchan Aruch* that is not already in one of these source writings, even if he has often erred in their use and evaluation and committed negligence.

In the Translation sections of this book, I have, at any rate, indicated the individual Talmud passages on which the corresponding regulations of Karo (and Isserles) are mainly based—so that if we regard as the "Talmud" in a broader sense the entire literature related to its provisions, the layman can see that the *Shulchan Aruch* is also a genuine son of the Talmud, and that the Decisors, etc. have been the inspiration for him. Karo took exception to the Jewish laws that were dependent on the existence of the Temple in Jerusalem, and which Maimonides takes into account with regard to its reconstruction at the time of the Messiah. In general, he includes only the practical laws valid at the time, only occasionally including those which he only assumes might still be in use somewhere, or whose regulations he preferred to those of the present.

B. The *Shulchan Aruch* (likewise the Talmud) is not an "Institution" of the "Jewish religious community, existing with corporate rights within the federal territory" in the sense of §166 of the Reich Criminal Code.[1] Not even the Ten Commandments of the Christian Church or the Jewish religious community are to be regarded as an "institution" within the meaning of §166 of the Reich Criminal Code, according to the case law

[1] This paragraph reads: "Whoever gives offense by publicly blaspheming God in abusive statements, or who publicly insults one of the Christian churches or another religious community with corporate rights existing within the Federal territory or their institutions or customs, ...shall be punished with imprisonment for up to three years." Since 1881, Judaism has also been included in the above-mentioned religious associations by the Imperial Court.

of the Reich Court. This is even less the case with the Talmud, not to mention the *Shulchan Aruch.*[2] Both are not even textbooks—religious teachings are not protected by §166—but only communications about different doctrines, many of which were not generally accepted at all, others only temporarily.

C. The opinion of contemporary Judaism on the *Shulchan Aruch* is not uniform. In Judaism there is no unconditional religious or human religious-legal authority on the teachings, as for example, the pope in the Catholic Church. Nor is there a fundamental "confessional writing", like the Apostles' Creed for the Christian Churches or the Augsburg Confession (1530) for the Protestant, or the "*Canones et decreta*" (Doctrines and Decisions) of the Tridentine Council (1564) for the Catholic Church. As the great Jewish Talmudist and philosopher Maimonides summarized the quintessence of the Jewish faith in his "Thirteen Articles," he experienced fierce opposition, and the "Articles" were by no means accepted as authoritative.

Two important points follow:

1. Orthodox Judaism views the *Shulchan Aruch* (with both Karo and Isserles), together with the authoritative commentaries on it, as its religious law.

The average Orthodox rabbi is content with the *Shulchan Aruch* and, for example, the remarks of a commentary printed with his edition. Cf.

---

[2] In my multiple activities as a court expert, I got to see, among other things, the following effort by an apparently still quite young, overzealous public prosecutor (enriched by leaflets, etc. from the "Central Association of German Citizens of the Jewish Faith") to bring down the all too harsh judgment of the *Schulchan Aruch* and the Talmud through the following Talmudic summer logic: The *Schulchan Aruch* is based on the Talmud, the Talmud on the Old Testament, Judaism also on the Old Testament; consequently, an "insult" against the *Schulchan Aruch* is also an "insult" against Jewish society, existing with corporate rights within the federal territory, consequently to be punished according to § 166 StGB! Unfortunately, to my knowledge, this product of the mind has not attained appreciation by the Imperial Court. I am therefore at this point saving it for posterity.

Graetz, *History of the Israelites* IX, 2nd Ed., p. 133: "The *Shulchan Aruch* forms to this day for [orthodox-minded] German and Polish Jews the religious norm, the official Judaism, and whatever that includes." Likewise for Russian and other European Orthodox Jews, in short, for about 80% of all Jewry. Here in Germany, due to the post-war mass immigration of Russian and other Orthodox "Jews from the East", and even earlier in North America though immigration, the number of followers of the *Shulchan Aruch* has increased considerably. The Frankfurter Rabbi Dr. Cäsar Seligmann (*History of the Jewish Reform Movement.* Frankfurt a.M. 1922, S. 17) claims that Orthodox Judaism had "gradually ceased to be the religion of the vast majority of the Jews of Western Europe and the New World", and that "official Judaism" has gradually become for modern Jewry "a religion of books, a mere doctrine, from which life has turned away."

It does not seem right to me, first of all, if the "Old Believer" German Jews are contrasted with an "immense majority" of foreign non-Orthodox Jews, whose "monstrosity" in many cases consists in the fact that they are only mere Jews in name, who indeed, have their sons circumcised and probably also "confirmed" [bar mitzvah] (which no Jew on earth refrains from doing, even if he himself is the most incredulous and indifferent), because they still have to pay Jewish municipal taxes, but otherwise do not care the least about Judaism as a religious phenomenon, but only, to allude to the early baptized Jew Karl Marx, to serve their worldly God, money.[3]

---

[3] Marx writes: "Let us consider the real, secular Jew, not the Sabbath Jew! … Let us not seek the secret of the Jew in his religion, but the secret [of this] religion in the real Jew! What is the worldly foundation of Judaism? The practical need, the self-interest? What is the worldly cult of the Jew? The haggler! What is his worldly god? Money! … The Jew has emancipated himself in a Jewish way, not only by appropriating the power of money, but in that through him …Money has become the world's power and the practical Jewish spirit has become the spirit of the Christian peoples. The Jews have emancipated themselves insofar as the Christians have become Jews. Money is the zealous God of Israel, before whom no other God may exist. The God of the Jews has become the world God; change [however] is the real God of the Jews." Karl Marx, the socialist prophet (1813-1883), was the son of a Jewish lawyer from Trier, "who had his whole family baptized for the sake of his career".

Furthermore, Seligmann does not seem to know that it is not only East German Jewish communities that have received an essential "push to the right" in cult and customs as a result of the influx of Eastern Jews. Moreover, in communities that had adopted Seligmann's German, genuinely poetic, substitute for the strange "Kol nidré", the "Kol nidré" formula reappears—and that, e.g., in contrast to the earlier, moderately liberal rabbis, Dr. Goldschmidt and Dr. Porges, his successor in Leipzig does not allow his children to attend public schools, write on the Sabbath, and is therefore conducting a lawsuit. Eastern Jewish Orthodox influence is also said to be making itself felt in some Berlin communities and synagogues. Incidentally, Seligmann himself speaks of "the immense majority of the old Orthodox Jewry in Eastern European countries, who have not yet been touched by the waves of modern education." This immense majority still teaches, thinks, and lives completely and faithfully according to the *Shulchan Aruch*!

2. Liberal (Reform) Judaism, which exhibits various tendencies, has allegedly turned away from the *Shulchan Aruch.*

This can be seen most sharply in the "Guidelines for a Program for Liberal Judaism," elaborated by the (since 1889 existing) "German Association of Liberal Rabbis" and approved in 1912 by the Posen General Assembly of the "Association for Liberal Judaism". However, the extraordinarily radical "Guidelines" beat all similar pronouncements of an extreme tendency of other confessions by many lengths, and leave traditional Judaism with almost only the outer shell. This shell, as Goethe would say, is filled with "the Lord's own spirit", so that one, who has dealt extensively with Judaism, often really has the impression with Cahn of "foreign views with Jewish markers". There is, of course, naturally no room for the content and spirit of the *Shulchan Aruch.*

But... in view of these "Guidelines," some questions are justified:

(a) If, according to "Guidelines" IV (Seligmann, p. 157), "the Holy Scriptures" [read: The Old Testament], as well as the further development of Judaism in post-biblical writings, the Talmud, rabbinical writings [thus also the *Shulchan Aruch*!] and the religious and philosophical literature up to the present" are no more than a mere "historical foundation for the Jewish religion"—how did the gentlemen Liberal rabbis, file criminal charges based on §166 of the Criminal Code, sign as "experts" to declare the paragraph in question violated, if, for example, the Talmud, the *Shulchan Aruch*, etc. had been "reviled"? It is just as little their business, as if I were to revile the Roman *Corpus Juris Civilis*, which to a large extent forms the "basis" of our Civil Code, and that I would then be denounced, accused, and examined as a reviler of the Civil Code!

And, as if such "historical foundations of the Jewish religion" should also include those that have come into being "up to the present", then the latest "development of Judaism", namely, the "Guidelines," would probably be sacrosanct as well. And should an Orthodox Jewish or Christian critic, who subjected this elaboration to the most sever scientific or even ethical censorship, he would ultimately fall under §166 "for insulting the Jewish religious community" or even one of its "institutions," if the "Guidelines" be assessed as such? Because according to "Guidelines" XII, the fact the "German Association of Liberal Rabbis" advocates for the religious unity of Judaism, it is thereby endowed by a magical act "and therefore (!) the assertion of denominational differences within Judaism is untrue"; consequently the lying press has attacked "religiously united" Judaism with the "guidelines", their spiritual fathers and godparents, and §166 StGB. comes at him quick as a flash under the blessing of congenial "experts".

May the Orthodox rabbis and other Jews also defend themselves against such "religious unity" with the gentleman Liberals, where and how they can, and the unbiased expert non-Jew (perhaps with some less well-known expert exceptions) can shake his head in the name of truth and logic, and say with Horace: "*Credat Judaeus Apella*".[4]

One sees: The aforesaid Liberal rabbinical association has indeed let go of the old Judaism, but not of the old Jewish spirit of revenge, and knew how to keep open for itself, the "Central Association" and other authorities, the way to §166 StGB. Obvious fallacies, which are also recognizable to their originators and untrue accusations of untruth are always the sign of a bad defense of a bad cause, even if the mis-logician can easily mislead Jewish and non-Jewish know-nothings (to which

[4] Ed.: The full phrase is "*Credat Judaeus Apella, non ego*" ("The Jew Apella may believe it, but not me"), from Horace, *Satire* I.5, 100, circa 35 BC.

Judges, etc. can belong) with it. The *Shulchan Aruch* is so unfashionable as to forbid the "stealing of a person's senses through words"—i.e. misleading by words that can, at any rate, be interpreted otherwise! There are certainly many among the Liberal rabbis and laymen who still fully agree with the *Shulchan Aruch* in this respect.

(b) If the Old Testament, the Talmud, the "Codices" including the *Shulchan Aruch* and all possible other "further developments of Judaism up to the present" form only 'the historical basis" ("Guidelines" IV)—if, furthermore, "Judaism, as a historical religion" [read: a phenomenon] "has given various expressions to its respective forms of development", and if, according to the view of liberal Judaism, "every period of Judaism", by virtue of the idea of development, "has the right and the duty, while preserving its essential (?) content, to abandon historically conditioned beliefs and manifestations, to develop them further, or to create new ones" ("Guidelines" V)—if all this is true, then...

Where is the epitome of this crown of creation, of modern liberal Judaism, to be found? What then is "the doctrinal content of the Jewish religion" from which "beliefs that cloud the purity of the Jewish idea of God are to be eliminated"? Who then has formulated this "purity" in liberal Judaism? Where is it written? Who or what decides which of the "many traditional idea, institutions, and customs" that "have disappeared from consciousness and from life, and thus have lost their content and meaning?" Who then decides about which "ideas do not correspond to the conditions", and therefore, "have no obligatory force"? Who and what decides further about "what disturbs the dignified celebration of the Sabbath and ... feasts", and therefore "shall be considered forbidden", and which "aggravations of the commandment to rest [on the Sabbath] have no claim to validity"? —Where then is "the new way" described, with which "the solemn customs" of the Sabbath candle lighting, the "parental blessing" (Kaddish?), the Seder (= Passover) evening, etc., "should be surrounded"? — Where is it stipulated how "the form of ritual divorce is to be settled? —Where and how is the contradiction balanced between "Guidelines" IX 3a (according to which "belonging to Judaism is given by birth") and "Guidelines" X (according to which only one who meets the "essential requirements" of "Guidelines" IX and X suffices" "to be regarded as a Jew")? —Where is the new "*Shulchan Aruch*" of liberal

Judaism, which supposedly constitutes its "religious unity", so that an expert or "expert" has a point of reference for assessing what is currently considered to apply as concepts, institutions, and customs of Jewish religious society, existing with corporate rights within the [German] federal territory"?

Oh no, "a position is still to be taken on this", since "the development" is yet "taking place in the present"! At least for the time being, what role should such a modern, liberal Jewish Religious Codex play? For example, Kohler's Systematic Theology of Judaism" or J. Goldschmidt's "The Being of Judaism", which Cahn has so pitilessly mauled? Or any other "representation" of the "doctrines, institutions and customs". Or did Rabbi Dr. Cäser Seligman already have this modern "*Shulchan Aruch*" lying on the desk? Or is every liberal rabbi free to decide what modern Judaism is according to the said paragraph? — Cahn wrote his above-named accounts with Kohler and Goldschmidt specifically to prove "that a religious communion between 'Reformed' [liberal Judaism] and [genuine] Judaism is not possible".

What about Seligmann's notion of the "religious unity" of Judaism, which, of course for our inexperienced jurists, is just an idea that is as constant as it is false? The congregations of Orthodox Jews, who want to know even less about this problematic notion of "religious unity" with the Liberals, than they would want to know about the cross and baptismal water, do yet also "exist" in defiance of Seligmann, "with corporate rights within the federal territory" as just such a "religious society" as the liberal ones! And they have a real, defiantly positive religious right in the real old *Shulchan Aruch*, contrary to all subjectively-experienced "developments" and concessions to the zeitgeist! You can point your finger at the individual places, not just in the air, where "a sea of blue thoughts" of Jewish liberal origin floats, according to rabbinic opinion, like an army of certain shadowless beings "in the air of the world".

(c) A third question also arises: Can the liberal new Jews ("*Minusjuden*" [Lesser Jews] say the Orthodox) really do without the *Shulchan Aruch* as completely as they appear to? Oddly, there is nothing about slaughter in the "Guidelines". It can be perhaps assumed, however, that the liberal rabbis and more serious laypeople, at least, do not eat "trimmed" or "nabbed" (unclean or improperly slaughtered) animals, but rather "kosher" animals (clean and properly slaughtered according to ritual). Is the information in the butcher's booklets enough for you about all these things? And if so, what are they based on? On the *Shulchan Aruch*! The *Shulchan Aruch* not only plays the role of a mere "historical basis", but is also still quite energetically normative for the liberal "Guideline" Jews!

Even the most ultra-liberal Jew unconditionally has his male child circumcised, if possible, on the 8th day after birth. Since descent from Jewish parents brings about natural membership in Judaism, circumcision, as with the Arabs, etc., could only take place later in boyhood. Why does the liberal Jew also have the little ones circumcised on the 8th day? Because the Torah, the Talmud and *Shulchan Aruch* command it so, not merely mentioning it as "historical foundations"! Is it done by modern Jews, by means of a doctor according to the rules of modern surgery and hygiene? No, as far as I know, the Jewish liberals still use the community official for circumcision (the local "Mohel") while practicing the old, barbaric *priah* (uncovering the glans by tearing off the incised foreskin), etc. entirely according to the *Shulchan Aruch*! Here, too, this is still more than a mere "historical foundation"! [That in Germany, on the modernist side, in some places, the Mohel is *no longer allowed to suck the circumcision blood by mouth* (!), but rather by means of a small glass tube containing sterilized cotton wool, cf. my "Blood in Jewish Literature and Custom".] It would lead too far, however, to mention more. The reader sees enough in any case, that the *Shulchan Aruch*, thrown out of the Jewish liberal cultural salon over the front steps, just as Horace says (*Epistles* I 10:24): "Drive out nature with the pitchfork, yet she always returns".[5]

(d) Do the spiritual fathers, who have their say in the "Guidelines", and the approving community representatives of extremely "Liberal" Reformed Jews, really believe that they have banished the spirit of the Talmud and the *Shulchan Aruch* by officially rejecting or sharply curtailing the objectionable old Talmud and the regulations of the *Shulchan Aruch*, which still live on undisturbed even in liberal Judaism, in spite of all the nice words of reform? The spirit of the *Shulchan Aruch* is the spirit of the 'Halachic' Talmudists. The nearly thousand-year-old influence of the

---

[5] Ed.: The point being that Reform Jews can "drive out" the Talmud and *Shulchan Aruch*, but they inevitably return in the soul of the Jew. Reform Jews are still governed by those precepts.

Talmud on Judaism, as well as the approximately five-hundred-year-old disciplining of Jewish thought and action by the *Shulchan Aruch*, can no more be resolved away in the Jewish people's soul within a few years or decades than the even older influence of the New Testament on the Christian people, or the influence of Luther on the Protestant mentality. Such real "Guidelines" of thinking, feeling, and acting, inherited from generation after generation, not on paper, but in unwearied flesh and blood, continue to have an effect just as unconsciously, but also just as surely as if the person guided by them consciously carried out the corresponding instructions.[6]

"Reformers" have existed in Judaism since the oldest times, and they were mostly (like Dr. Seligmann and his comrades) inspired by the most laudable intentions. Under the same rejection of the Talmud and the *Shulchan Aruch* as the still prevailing normative codes of law, some have made up an "ideal Mosaicism", which is supposed to correspond to the spirit of today's time, but unfortunately (according to Goethe) it is "only the Lord's own spirit" (Marx-Dalman, "Jewish Foreign Law") and even goes so far as to exchange the Sabbath with Sunday and to deny the necessity of circumcision.

But the standard for this, as well as for what is to be eliminated, is purely subjective, and could ultimately lead to as many "Judaisms" as there are Jews, or even to a dissolution of Judaism—because there would be less of a boundary, while, as mentioned, Judaism has no generally recognized "confessional writing" (like e.g. Catholics and Protestants) that at least defines immovably the characteristic features of the corresponding concept of faith.

---

[6] It is therefore mostly absurd when careless writers (especially editors), speakers, etc. write or say that these or those crimes committed by a Jew are "commanded in the Talmud (or *Shulchan Aruch*)" or are "prescribed". In very special cases, one could at the most say: "The deed of the accused almost looks as if he had, half or quite unconsciously, been inspired by these or those views of the Talmud (or decisions of the *Shulchan Aruch*)," or: "the deed shows a strange resemblance to this or that view or story in the Talmud (or *Shulchan Aruch*)." Racial psychologists would attribute such obscure perpetuation of ancient norms to racial- or blood-inheritance. Thus, in the "*Berliner Börsen-Courier*" of 5 July 1913, the Jewish writer Kauder explained that the literary judgment he made there about the Cabbalah was "not at all controlled by any specific knowledge", but was limited to "a simple understanding of blood."

Any ‘reform’ that is too harsh, like any revolution, is bound to provoke a reaction. The Hellenistic assimilationists were followed by the Maccabees, the Mendelssohnian assimilationists by the neo-Orthodox in the direction of Samson Raphael Hirsch, and in contrast to all liberal rabbis, together with the lay assemblies and their declarations and resolutions, the “communal orthodoxy” is an effective authority, which considers the, albeit in places crumbling, Talmudic-rabbinic beams of a “moderately” administered *Shulchan Aruch* to be more “sustainable” than the shaky network of the various “modern Judaisms” offered for selection today.

In short: even in liberal Judaism today—even contrary to external denial[7]—not only the spirit, but also the form of the *Shulchan Aruch* is of far-reaching effectiveness and its aura as a genuine descendant of the Talmud is by no means extinguished.

---

[7] A Catholic clergyman once said: “Some people may play the libertine on the beer bench or with their girlfriends (particularly non-believers): but at Easter time they still come obediently to the confessional and to communion, and they desire the last rites for themselves and their own all the more. The Christian heart is stronger than the loose mouth.” The same applies to the “free-thinking” Jews, Protestants, and “atheists”.

— 4 —

TRANSLATIONS (1): ORACH CHAYIM

Since it is impossible to translate the entire *Shulchan Aruch* within the framework of this book, I have elected to include here a few longer passages from the first part of the *Shulchan Aruch* (Orach Chayim) in context, in order to show the whole character and layout of this work. But mostly, I decode and discuss those individual passages that have become the subject of the heated controversy about the *Shulchan Aruch*. This gives a scientifically accurate translation of individual, shorter passages from the *Shulchan Aruch* that played a role in the polemics and apologetics on the occasion of the so-called "*Judenspiegel*", together with my explanations. Included here are passages from Karo's text, along with (as appropriate) the commentary ('*Hagah'*) of Isserles—which, again, is accepted as a formal part of the full *Schulchan Aruch.*

Orach Chayim 2. Of Dressing Early.

1. "Do not put your shirt on while sitting down, but take it and put your head and arms into it while still lying down, so that you are already covered with it when you stand up." [Talmud, Shabbat 118a]

2. "One does not say: 'I am inside a room (alone); who can see me there?' [and take offense at my base upper body? Talmud, Hagigah 17a, Ta'anit 11b]. This is because all the Earth is full of the glory of the Holy, Blessing of God (Isaiah 6:3)."

3. "One takes care to put on his shirt properly, so that the inside is not turned inside out." [Talmud, Shabbat 114a.]

4. "Put on the right shoe first, but do not tie it: then put on the left shoe and tie it first; then tie the right shoe." [Talmud Shabbat 61a.]. *Hagah*: "With shoes that have no laces, one puts on the right one first."

5. “When taking off one’s shoes, take off the left one first.” [Shabbat 61a]

6. “It is forbidden to walk proudly with one’s head raised or even for four cubits with one’s head uncovered.” [Talmud, Berakhot 43a]. And one is mindful of the performance of his need to relieve oneself.” [Berakhot 15b; and, transition to §3 below!]. *Hagah*: “One covers one’s whole body with clothing [apart from the head] and does not go barefoot. [Talmud, Shabbat 129b.]. Also, one gets into the habit of relieving oneself in the morning and in the evening; for this is part of order and cleanliness.”

Orach Chayim 3. Behavior in the Toilet.

1. “When you go to the toilet, say: ‘Be praised, Honored one!’ Nowadays, however, it is not common to say it.

2. “One should be modest in the toilet and only expose oneself when one has sat down.” [Talmud, Berakhot 62a.]. *Hagah*: “It is not permitted for two men to go to the toilet together, nor may one speak, and the privy door must be closed for reasons of modesty.”

3. “If one wants to touch the opening of the anus with a potsherd or a piece of kindling in order to hasten the emptying, one should touch it before sitting down, but not when one already sat down, because otherwise one runs the risk of being bewitched.” [Talmud, Berakhot 62a]

4. “A man should not expose himself more than one span high [about 9 inches] in the rear, and two spans high in the front, but a woman only one span high behind, but not at all in the front.” [Talmud, Berakhot 23a; because in the case of the man, contamination of the kaftan in the front is otherwise possible by urine shaking off at the same time.]

5. “When defecating in an open, unenclosed place, be sure that it is done facing north and with the back to the south, or vice versa; it is forbidden to sit between the east and the west (so that one’s back is turned toward Jerusalem).” [Talmud Berakhot 61a]. *Hagah*: “However, shaking urine off is permissible in any direction.”

6. "And likewise, it is forbidden for a man to sleep between east and west when his wife lies with him [Talmud, Berakhot 60b.]. But he should also avoid this if his wife does not sleep with him."

7. "Whoever shakes urine off in front of an attendant should not face the Temple, or he shall leave the temple to the side." [Talmud, Berakhot 61a.]

8. "If one (wants to) relieve oneself in a field, he may do so immediately if he does so behind a fence: but in an open field you must go as far from the path as possible, so that no other Jew can see the exposure." [Talmud, Berakhot 62c.]

9. "One should not sit down quickly and forcefully, nor should one exert oneself more than necessary, so as not to tear one's anal sphincter." [Talmud, Shabbat 82a.]

10. "One must not wipe oneself with their right hand." [Talmud, Berakhot 62a; because with the right hand, one ties one's phylacteries[1], brings food to the mouth, beats time with one's right hand while reading the Holy Scriptures like a song, and because God gave the Mosaic law with his right hand, as it is read out in Deuteronomy 33:2.]

11. "One should not wipe oneself with a disc of clay, because of the danger of being enchanted, nor with hay, because the sphincter is weakened if one wipes oneself with a combustible object." [Talmud, Shabbat 82a.]

Hagah: "Nowadays, however, when the toilets are not in the field, it is customary to wipe oneself with a clay disk; it is also customary to wipe oneself with a combustible object [hay or paper], without being harmed in doing so. Incidentally, one follows the customs of the people."

12. "One relieves oneself at night just as modestly as during the day." [Talmud, Berakhot 62a.]

---

[1] Or 'Tefillin': a small leather box, worn on the body, which contains holy texts.

13. One should not shake off the urine standing upright, because urine will be splashed on your feet, unless you are on a high place, or if you shake it off on dusty earth." [Talmud, Niddah 13a.]

14. "One should be careful while shaking off urine, that one does not touch the penis except where the glans begins, because otherwise a useless discharge of semen may occur. A married man may indeed touch his penis; but it is the religious custom to be cautious, even when one is married." [Niddah 13a.]

15. "Even if one is not married, it is permissible to support the testicles with the hand." [Niddah 13a.]

16. "Even a married man is not permitted to touch the penis, except when he shakes off urine; on the other hand, it is also not permitted to scratch it."

17. "Whoever delays the relief of their own need breaks the prohibition (of Leviticus 20:25): 'Do not defile yourselves'." [Talmud, Makkot 16b.]

Orach Chayim 55,20

> "If ten Jews are together in one place and say Kaddish or Kedushah prayers, one who is not with them [but at a distance] can also say the word 'Amen'. Some say: it is permitted if neither feces nor anything non-Jewish separates them."

The Jew, who happens to be apart, may only participate in the prayers of the "minyan" if nothing impure separates him from it. The distasteful pairing of 'non-Jews' and 'excrement' is not meant to disparage the Gentiles.

Orach Chayim 113,8

> "If a Jew is praying, and someone comes towards him with a cross in his hand, but the Jew comes to a point in the prayer text where it is customary to bow, he should *not* bow, although his heart thinks of heaven."

It could otherwise look as if the Jew was paying homage to the cross. According to Isserles (Yoreh De'ah 141,1 *Hagah*), the cross is something idolatrous; the bowing Jew would thus appear to be worshipping a cult symbol (religious symbol) that was "idolatrous" for him. Because Isserles says in his *Hagah* (which is absolutely equal to the main text of the *Shulchan Aruch*) in Yoreh De'ah 141,1; "The form of a cross, before which one bows, is equal to an idol and is forbidden".

Orach Chayim 158. On Wetting the Hands before the Midday Meal[2]

1. "When one is about to eat bread, over which one has said the saying, 'Thou bring forth bread out of the earth', wet the hands before—even if one is unaware of any previous contamination of them. And speak the blessing that ends with the words: '...about the moistening of the hands'. [Talmud, Hagigah 18b.] But with bread over which the blessing 'Thou bring forth' is *not* said—e.g. biscuit and toast, which do not form a proper meal but are eaten along with it—hand-wetting is not necessary."

2. "Someone says that, with a piece of bread about the size of an egg, one should wet one's hands, but not say a blessing."

3. "If one eats a piece of bread less than the size of an olive, one is not, as some say, required to wet the hands."

4. "If one eats something [such as vegetables or fruit] that you dip into one of the following liquids[3] as a condiment—namely, *Jàjin* [wine], *debâsch* [honey], *schèmen* [oil], *chèleb* [milk], *tal* [dew], ***dâm* [blood]** and *màjjim* [water]—then one must wet the hands, but without the usual

[2] Note: It is not a matter of washing the hands in our sense, nor of immersing the hands, but pouring water over the hands as a symbol of *ritual purification.*
[3] An edible (and lawful to eat) object can appear unclean if it has been moistened by one of the seven liquids listed (Talmud, Mishnah Makhshirin VI, 4). Therefore, one must wet one's hands with water before eating vegetables or fruits, even if the vegetables or fruits are immersed in one of the liquids, because otherwise the hands, considered impure before wetting, would make the food forbidden.

blessing, if one eats it, and must do so before those liquids have dried on it" [Talmud, Temurah XI, 2; Makhshirin VI, 4; Hullin 33a.].

Hagah: "And even if one has dipped only the top of the vegetable or fruit in such a liquid, one must wet the hands with water, yet without any benediction." [Talmud, Pesahim 115b.]

Commentary: *The consumption of blood is allowed in the Shulchan Aruch!* Karo seems to think nothing of it, and his commentator Isserles does not apply a "Hagah" to this striking rule! Only the author of the commentary *Magén Abraham*, who died in 1682, says that blood as a diet is only permitted for a dangerously ill person for whom his doctor has prescribed the consumption of blood!

The otherwise conscientious Strack, who collected even the remotest trifles on the "blood question" in his well-known book *The Blood*, passed by this point; certain so-called "experts" on Jewish or non-Jewish blood still swear, with enviable light-heartedness, that "Jewish religious law absolutely forbids any consumption of blood". The truth is the following: The Old Testament (Lev 17:10ff., cf. 3:17; 7:26f.; 19:26; Deut 12:16 and 23, as well as 1 Sam 14:22ff.) and also the Acts of the Apostles (15:29) only forbid the consumption of the blood of *cattle and birds*—primarily of those used for sacrifices. This, according to Lev 17:10ff., on the grounds that the blood is destined, to be offered certainly as a means of expiation, to the Lord alone. The Old Testament allows for other consumption of blood.

Incidentally, the Old Testament threatens the forbidden consumption of blood, not with legal, but rather divine punishment ("extermination", i.e. premature death). Maimonides says in his *Jad Chasakah* in the section *Màachalôth asurôth* (Forbidden Foods) VI, 1f.:

> "Whoever deliberately eats as much blood as an olive, has forfeited his salvation; if done intentionally, he is culpable for a sin offering. The guilt occurs only with the blood *of animals* and birds, whether domestic or wild, whether clean or unclean. *On the other hand, there is no indebtedness in the blood of fish, locusts, reptiles, amphibians, and human blood* [because none of this blood is mentioned in the Bible!]. It is therefore lawful to eat the blood of clean fish and

> to drink it, once it has been collected into a vessel. The blood of unclean fish and locusts, like the milk of unclean cattle, is forbidden only because it forms part of their (unclean) body; for the same reason the blood and flesh of reptiles is forbidden.
>
> Human blood is [not mentioned in the Bible, and] rabbinically forbidden [only] when separated from the body; whoever disobeys that will be beaten. One may swallow blood from the gums [because it is not yet "separated from the body" in the mouth]. But if one has bitten into bread and found blood on it (from the gums), one scrapes off the blood, because it is now separated from the body, and only then eats the bread."

Somewhat differently, the *Shulchan Aruch* (Yoreh De'ah 66,1) says: "The blood of tame and wild animals as well as birds is forbidden, whether they are pure or impure". And in §9: "The blood of fish [because the Old Testament does not forbid it] is in itself permitted, but collected in a vessel, it may not be consumed if it can be mistaken for other [e.g. forbidden animal] blood; on the other hand, its consumption is permissible if it is recognizable as fish blood, e.g. if there are scales in it". And in §10 [in the uncensored text]: "Human blood, if separated from the body, is forbidden because of its appearance [because it could be mistaken for animal blood that is Biblically forbidden]. Therefore, whoever eats bread, they must first remove any blood that may have come out of the gums; but if the blood is still between their teeth, one may swallow it".[4]

5. "Whoever wets his hands before enjoying fruit, he is one of the haughty." [Talmud, Hagigah 18b, Hullin 106a.]. *Hagah*: This applies only if he wets them as if it were an obligatory commandment; but if he wets them only for the sake of cleanliness, because they are unclean, it is permitted.

---

[4] Ed.: This whole point is hugely significant for the 'blood libel' debate over the centuries, in which many non-Jews have argued that Jews in fact continued (and perhaps even today) to use human blood in ritual ceremonies or as a dietary or health practice. Jews have longed denied it, but their own text, along with historical evidence, is damning. For details on the history, see A. Toaff, *Passovers of Blood* (2020; T. Dalton, ed.).

Roasted meat, as is evident from the words of a scholar, falls under the same provision as fruit [i.e. one does not wet one's hands before eating it], even if it is moistened by meat juice. A dish prepared from wheat, which is dry, also falls under this provision."

6. "Before drinking, one need not wet even one hand." [Thosaphoth to Talmud, Hagigah 18b].

7. "If one has wetted his hands in order to eat something that he dips in a liquid [see above], and one then wants to eat bread, it is evident from the words of a scholar, that for this bread, this earlier wetting is not sufficient, and all the less if one has first wetted his hands without intending to eat bread and only then decides to eat." [Talmud, Hagigah 18b, Hullin 31 a,b.]. *Hagah*: "However, unless one diverts one's attention from the hands, one wets them without blessing. If one touches the unclean parts of the body while eating, one must wet one's hands again."

8. "Whoever is in a desert or a dangerous place and has no water, is exempt from hand wetting." [Talmud, Eruvin 17a.]

9. "It is necessary to pay close attention to the wetting the hands, for whoever takes it lightly is guilty of banishment, comes into poverty, and is removed from the world." [Talmud, Eduyot V, 6 (Mishnah) Shabbat 62a, Sotah 4b.]

10. "Although a quarter log [about two ounces] is enough, take more for wetting, for Rab Chisda says [in the Talmud]: 'I use plenty of water for wetting my hands, and God blessed me for this with full hands!'" [Talmud, Shabbat 62b.]

11. "Say the blessing before wetting the hands, because, with all the commandments, the blessing is said before it is carried out. But it is also customary to say the blessing after wetting them, because the hands are sometimes not clean. One says the blessing only after shaking off the water that has been poured on the hands for the first time, so that the hands are clean before pouring water on them a second time." [Talmud, Pesahim 7b, 119a.]

12. “One should dry the hands well before breaking bread; for eating with hands that are not dried is like eating unclean bread.” [Talmud, Sotah 4b.]

Orach Chayim 330-332

330,1 “An expecting Jewish woman is like a sick person in mortal danger, and because of her, one desecrates the Sabbath with regard to everything that she needs [by performing otherwise forbidden acts]. One calls [e.g.] for a midwife from one place or another, one performs her [complete] midwifery, a light is turned on for her, even if she is blind”.[5]

330,2. “One does not assist at the birth of a non-Jewish woman on the Sabbath, even by something [an act], in which there is no profanation of the Sabbath.”

332,1. “One does not assist at a birth of a domestic animal on the Sabbath”.[6]

---

[5] Otherwise, as is well known, lighting candles on the Sabbath is forbidden to the Jew, so that very devout Eastern Jews on the Sabbath do not even dare to press an electric bell, because a tiny spark is evoked on contact! Sabbath dishes must already be cooked on Friday and are only kept warm until the Sabbath; as a result, the Jews became the inventors of the first “cooking boxes”. As is well-known, a compliant non-Jew (*Shabbos-Goy*) or a non-Jewess (*Shabbos-Goite*) may be entrusted with all work forbidden to the Jews on the Sabbath.

[6] The provisions are taken from the Talmud. 1. Mishnah Shabbat XVIII 3 (= sheet 128b): “One may not provide [full] midwifery to a pet on the feast day, but one may provide assistance. One may provide midwifery to a [Jewish] woman on the Sabbath, including a midwife for her to call from one place to another [for childbirth] and [otherwise] desecrate the Sabbath for her [the woman giving birth] and [e.g.] tie the umbilical cord; Rabbi Jose says: also cut [the cord].” [Gemara] 128b: “How is the assisting done [with the pregnant domestic animal]? … One grasps the [emergent] fruit so that the fruit comes out [etc.] One may assist a [Jewish] woman in childbirth on the Sabbath. … If she needs a light, a friend will light a candle for her; if she needs oil, a friend will bring it to her: [etc.].

2. Mishnah Avodah Zarah II 1 (= 26): “A Jewess may not help a non-Jewess [at all] in childbirth, if other [Jewish women] are present, but not when both [Jewess and non-Jewess] are alone together. … Rab Joseph wanted to say that on the Sabbath one would help a non-Jew give birth, but for a fee, because

Orach Chayim 605,1. The Chicken Sacrifice of the Eve of the Day of Atonement

> "As for the custom on the eve of the Day of Atonement of slaughtering a rooster as a sin offering for each male, and saying certain phrases over him, there are scholars who forbid this custom."
>
> *Hagah*: "There are Geonim who write of this custom, and likewise many later authorities write about it. It is maintained in all modern-day countries and should not be changed, because it has become firmly established. It is

---

[otherwise] enmity [against the Jews] could arise. Abajé replied: One can refuse [midwifery] and say: For our wives who keep the Sabbath, we may profane the Sabbath; but for your wives who do not keep the Sabbath, we must not profane the Sabbath." In contrast to the more humane position of at least some Talmudists, who want to allow childbirth assistance for domestic animals and paid birthing assistance for non-Jews even on the Sabbath, the *Shulchan Aruch* inhumanely forbids both on the Sabbath and in this respect, [indirectly] equates the non-Jewess with the female domestic animal.

In Orach Chayim 512,1-3, it is said that the Jew should not invite a non-Jew to his place on one of his feast days and so on account of this he should cook more. ... On the other hand, one may cook a little more for one's own dogs in one's own pot on the feast day and give it to them to eat, even if one has something else for them that one could have given to them after all. The regulation is taken from the Talmud (Bézah 21b), where the reason is also given: It is up to the Jew to feed his dogs, but not to feed the non-Jew.

This does not mean that the non-Jew is undervalued. For according to Isserles (on Orach Chayim 512,1) the Jew may send some of the banquet food in his house to a non-Jew, likewise to the servant or maid of the non-Jew, who is to fetch such food from the Jew, and he may also let a non-Jew, who happens to randomly appear, eat with him [the Jew in his house]. In truth, the *Shulchan Aruch* permits the Jew to lend money at interest to a non-Jew who borrows from him on a Jewish semi-festive day, because otherwise the non-Jewish customer might be lost to him; even to a non-Jew, who does not otherwise borrow from him, the Jew may lend to on the semi-festive day, if he uses the non-Jew's (pre-payable) interest for the week to make for himself a joyful celebration. "Law" 17 (Orach Chayim 576,3): "If there is a plague among the pigs, one should humble oneself before God [by fasting, etc.], because the internal structure of pigs is similar to that of humans; one should humble oneself even more when there is a plague among the gentiles, but not when there is one among the Jews [of a certain place]" based on the Talmud (Ta'anit 21b).

> customary to choose a rooster for every male and a hen for every female; for a pregnant woman one takes a rooster and a hen; [because] perhaps she will give birth to a boy. It is customary to choose white chickens, because it is said [Isaiah 1:18]: 'Although your sins be as red as crimson, yet they shall become white as snow'. One used to give these sacrificial chickens or their monetary value [afterward] to the poor. [But first it is slaughtered, and] before slaughtering one usually puts one's hand on the animal's head in the manner of the ancient sacrificial customs."

Commentary: Scheftelowitz says, regarding the meaning of the custom:

> "According to the Jewish faith, the fate of the man is sealed for the coming year on the Feast of Atonement. The sinful man earns...severe divine punishments, perhaps death. Therefore, on the day on which the Feast of Atonement begins [at around 6 o'clock in the evening], the Jew takes a chicken, which is meant to be the substitute for him; it shall die in place of him.... The animal [rooster or hen] is swung around the head three times... [T]his generally widespread custom has the name *Kapparot*" [Atonement].
>
> "In Bukovina, a pregnant Jewess takes a hen [for herself] and an egg in her hand during the *Kapparot*. The egg is for the child developing under her heart, of which one does not know to which sex it will belong, just as one does not know which sex the chick to be hatched from the egg will have." (cf. Hovorka and Kronfeld, *Comparative Folk Medicine*, 1908.)

So this is a contemporary custom, as has otherwise been confirmed to me from the Jewish side as well.

Furthermore, in his work *Marginal Notes on the Daily Prayerbook* (1909), A. Berliner testifies that the above chicken sacrifice still occurs in the Jewish prayer books used today: "Also the 'Kapparot transfer', which still figures in the prayer book (!) should finally be dropped. The first to do this is Dr. M. Sachs in his prayer book".

Although Rabbi Moses ben Nachman in France and Rabbi Solomon ben Adereth in Barcelona (both 13th century) as well as Joseph Karo in the 16th century rejected the Day of Atonement chicken sacrifice as pagan, it has remained so preserved to this day, based on the great authority of Gaon Hai (around 1000 AD), Rabbi Mordechai (13th century), Rabbi Jakob ben Asher (14th century), etc.—thus, already for around 1000 years!

Of course, modern-day Reformed Judaism no longer practices that chicken sacrifice, but the Jews of the *Shulchan Aruch* do, and they have increased in number enormously since the Russian Jewish immigration. You should not be surprised if laymen conclude as follows with regard to this bloody sacrificial ritual, which is still practiced today: 1. instead of the actual Jew to be sacrificed, a rooster is an "extremely effective substitute; 2. according to the much-cited statement of Antonius Margarita, son of the Chief Rabbi of Regensburg, "one should use an ape for such a thing, because it resembles a human being the most closely(!)"; and 3. If, according to rabbinic passages, non-Jews are indeed not full human beings like the Jews, but are rather like cattle (Talmud, Bava Metzia 114b,2—see appendix) and, despite their human appearances, only conduct themselves like apes compared to the fully human Jew (*Shenei Luchot HaBerit* 250b), then wouldn't a non-Jew be the "most effective" substitute?[7]

---

[7] Ed.: Again, this has important implications for blood libel and Jewish ritual murder more generally. Jewish logic suggests that the killing of a non-Jew, as a "substitute," can expiate Jewish sin!

— 5 —
TRANSLATIONS (2): YOREH DE'AH

Yoreh De'ah 2,1

> "Whatever a Gentile slaughters is carrion, even if he is a youth, and even if he is not an idolater, and even if other Jews have watched him do it".[1]

The Talmud (Hullin 13a): "Whatever a non-Jew slaughters is carrion and defiles the Jew who carries it" [according to Lev 11:28: 'Whoever carries carrion defiles his clothes,' etc.].

Maimonides, *Hilchôch màachalôth asurôth* IV, 1: "Anything that is not ritually slaughtered, is considered dead." I have quoted the Maimonides literally, so that one can see how Karo has taken much almost verbatim from him.

Yoreh De'ah 113, 1

> "Something that is not eaten raw, but that a Gentile has cooked, even if it is on the dishes and in the house of a Jew, is forbidden."

In the extra-canonical tract *Pirké*, Rabbi Elieser says it more sharply:

> "Every Jew who eats with an uncircumcised man does as much as if he were eating with a dog; for just as the dog is not circumcised, so also he who has a foreskin is not circumcised. And whoever touches the uncircumcised is as one touching a corpse, and whoever bathes with him is as one bathing with a leper; for they [the Gentiles] are as dead while they are still alive, as when they are dead as carrion in the field, and their prayer does not come before the holy,

[1] Ed.: By 'carrion' (or 'carcass') the Bible intends an unclean corpse.

> blessed God, and of them it says [Psalms 115:17]: 'The dead do not praise Yahweh'."

Yoreh De'ah 116,5

> "One should not put anything cooked nor any drink under the bed, even if it is covered with an iron lid."

Similarly in the Talmud (Pesahim 112a): "It has been handed down: The evil spirit rests on food and drinks under the bed (and defiles them), even if they are covered with an iron lid."

Yoreh De'ah 117,1

> "No thing that is forbidden in the Torah may be traded, although its enjoyment is permitted, if the thing is intended for eating... On the other hand, game, birds or fish accidentally or unintentionally caught in one's net, are forbidden to a Jewish hunter, so he may sell them to Gentiles.[2] Likewise, if an animal in his house accidentally becomes carrion (*Nebëlah*) or is injured..."
>
> *Hagah*: "Likewise it is also permitted to take these forbidden things for the debts of Gentiles, because this is to be regarded as a saving from their hands".[3]

Nebëlah means a (clean) animal that has not been slaughtered, but has died of its own accord, thus actually carrion, and the regulation, for example, not to give it to the Gentile, but rather to sell it, means a spiteful disregard for him.

In the Talmud, which knows the rules of slaughter, and even more so in the *Shulchan Aruch*, *Nebëlah* is understood as not ritually and correctly slaughtered (not "kosher"), but rather as *nabbled* ['incorrectly slaughtered']. *Trëphah* is understood as an animal recognized to be unclean by

[2] Compare Deut 14:21: "You shall not eat carrion; but you may give it to an alien or sell it to the non-Jew."

[3] Ed.: In other words, Jews can accept forbidden items from non-Jews as payment for debt, if that is the only option.

the discovery of an external or internal bodily defect, and therefore it is considered forbidden. Today, the Jews usually call any non-kosher food *treife*. The "carrion" (the *Nebëlah*) in the *Shulchan Aruch* sounds a little stronger in translation than it is meant to. The fact that it may be sold to non-Jews, because they do not have the Jewish food bans, entails the further thought that the *Nebëlah* is forbidden as an abomination for the Jew who thinks strictly in this respect, but it is good enough for the non-Jews, who are indifferent to this.

Yoreh De'ah 119, 8

> "A Jew who is suspected of eating forbidden things ... cannot be believed."

This is perhaps the most agreeable phrase in the whole *Shulchan Aruch*; our judges should memorize it very carefully!

Yoreh De'ah 120, 1

> "Whoever buys eating utensils of metal or glass from non-Jews, or internally tinned vessels, even if they are new, must immerse them in a tub of water or a size 40 well."

This prescription is based on a lengthy discussion in the Talmud (Avodah Zarah 75b.). In Yoreh De'ah 123,1—where wine touched by idolaters is forbidden for consumption—the reason given is not (as in Justus and Ecker) "because the wine in contaminated by the touch of the idolaters", but in the *Hagah* of Isserles expressly states: "because it is to be feared that such wine is destined for a drink offering to the idols."

Yoreh De'ah 139 ff

> 139,1: "Usage of idols is forbidden, both of themselves and of things in their service, of their adornments and things of sacrifice, all the same, whether made by a Gentile or a Jew." (From Talmud, Avodah Zarah 40a.)

139,11: "Garments with which the idolatrous priests are clothed when they go into the idol house are their personal adornment, not in adornment of the idols, and therefore no disuse is required of the garments. Some consider this to be required".[4]

Hagah: "But what they are clothed with [as with liturgical vestments] for idolatry itself is called adornment of idols, and must be made useless."

139,15: "Some say that it is permitted for Jews to sell non-Jewish books."

Hagah: "But some say it is forbidden to sell them if they are hymnals for idolatry; others say it is only forbidden to sell them to the priests, not to other Gentiles. But whoever is strict about this, blessings will come. Some also forbid them parchment and ink to write the books of their religious law. Also, some say it is forbidden to lend money for construction or decoration or for the (religious) service of houses of idolatry, e.g. incense pans. Anyone who refrains from doing so will be fortunate." [From Talmud, Nedarim 62a]. "Nor should one bind the books of the Gentiles, except the books of the judges and the scribes. But if there is fear of enmity [because of the refusal], then one may do it, but one should avoid it as far as possible."

Yoreh De'ah 141 and 150-151

141,1: "All the images that are located in villages are forbidden for trade, as they are made for idolatrous worship; but those that are in large cities are permitted, since they are decidedly made only for adornment, except when they stand at the gate of the city district and they show a replica of a hand with a staff, a bird, a ball, a sword, a crown, or a ring."

---

[4] The identification of the priestly vestments and the mention of the hymnals or other religious books, and, above all, the baptismal water (below), show that what is meant here by 'idolatry' is the Christian (Catholic) religion!

Hagah: "The form of a cross to which one bows is considered an idol and is forbidden, without being made useless. However, a cross that one hangs around the neck as a token of remembrance is not called an idol, and it is permissible."

150,3: "Before princes or priests who have a cross on their robes or bear an image (of saints, etc.) on their breast, one must not bow down or uncover the heads—except in such a way that the true meaning of the action is not recognized; e.g. one drops coins [if it comes to pass,] [and bends down for them accordingly], or one stands up [when they sit down], even before they approach, and likewise, one takes off one's head covering and bows, before they get there."

Commentary: Compare to Orach Chayim 113:8, in Part 4 above. Yoreh De'ah 141,1 (without the *Hagah*) is taken directly from the Talmud (Avodah Zarah 40b and 41a) with little change, where the "sculptures" are probably mainly pagan statues of gods and emperors that are worshiped, perhaps as early as 200 AD. Christian crosses or the statues of saints can also be meant, in large cities also, those are used to adorn buildings, i.e. non-worshipped images of this kind. The forbidden figures with staff, bird, etc. are interpreted as venerated symbolic figures of the Roman Empire. The *Shulchan Aruch* apparently understands this to mean partly the images of saints, angels, etc., that are adorned and glorified with the attributes of a bishop's staff, etc., and partly those not worshipped as saintly figures or crosses at or on city buildings. The *Hagah* of Isserles, who lived at the same time as Karo, shows that the main issue was the relationship to the Christian cross, of which, as an object of worship, any use (purchase for sale, etc.) was forbidden. However, that which was used as a necklace, etc. could be bought and sold. What is meant is probably women's jewelry or the like, because:

Yoreh De'ah 150,3 forbids only the honoring of a worn cross or image if it is a Christian religious symbol; and in Orach Chayim 113,8, even the appearance of such honoring.

The remedies given in the first passage, to feign reverence and thereby avoid punishment for disregarding the Roman Catholic religion, which was possible in the Middle Ages and even later, are basically harmless. Even a rigid Protestant could proceed in a similar manner towards images of saints, etc., in strictly Catholic areas.

From a purely ethical point of view, of course, such a concealment of inner disregard, even hatred, of a foreign religious custom by means of the appearance of outward respect is sheer hypocrisy. The *Shulchan Aruch* seems to feel this obscurely, since it does not use the otherwise popular expressions that this is done "for the sake of peace" or to avoid "desecration of the Name" (i.e. evil judgment of the Jews and their God by Gentiles).

> 151,1: "Things intended for an idolatrous purpose in a particular place are not to be sold to the idolaters of that place."
>
> *Hagah*: "Some say that it is lawful to sell Christians incense and other objects of their worship, since their belief is only *Shittûph* (joining a divine being to God the Father). … The prohibition on selling to the idolaters things that belong to their worship, applies only if they have no such things available or cannot buy them elsewhere. But if they can also buy them elsewhere, they may be sold anything. … It is forbidden to sell water to a Gentile Christian, knowing that he will make baptismal water from it".[5]

---

[5] There is no question that by "idolaters" is here meant Christians. Marx-Dalman writes,

> "Isserles … feels compelled to draw attention explicitly to the fact that a cross is an idol (Yoreh De'ah 141,1), that Christian song and prayer books must be regarded as requisite props of idolatry (Yoreh De'ah 139,15), and that baptismal water is intended for an idolatrous use (Yoreh De'ah 151,1). Unless it is proven that Karo and Isserles consider the worship of the cross to be compatible with a closer observance of the Noahide commandments [allegedly binding on non-Jews], the opposite must be assumed."

Even Hoffmann must admit "that wherever the *Shulchan Aruch*" speaks about idolatry, the Christian cult is also meant, without other mention; "All laws that aim to keep the Jews away from idolatry must therefore also be related to Christians". For Maimonides, Christians are idolaters in every respect. Also in

Yoreh De'ah 154,1-2

> 154,1: "A non-Jewish woman may not assist a Jewess in childbirth, in the event she is alone with her [in her home], even if she is experienced in midwifery. Nor may she suckle a Jewish child in her home, even if others [namely, Jewish women] stand by. But in a Jewish house, it is permitted to assist a Jewess in childbirth or to suckle a Jewish child, if others [i.e. Jews] stand by or go from time to time. However, one should not leave the Jewish child alone with her at night."

> 154,2: "A Jewess should not suckle the child of a non-Jew, not even for payment. Only if she has an overabundance of milk and this causes her pain is she allowed to suckle it."

Commentary: Both are taken from the Talmud, but with deviations and with the omission of the poisonous justifications and the rabbinic pettifoggery there. It says in the Talmud, (Avodah Zarah 26a),

> [Mishnah:] "A Jewess may not assist a Gentile woman in childbirth, because in doing so she helps bring a child into the world for idolatry, but one may let a Gentile woman assist a Jewess in childbirth.[6] A Jewess may not suckle the child of a non-Jew, but a non-Jew may suckle the child of a Jewess in her [the Jewess'] apartment."

> [Gemara:] "Our rabbis have handed down: A Jewess is not allowed to assist a non-Jew in childbirth, because in doing

---

the regulation of the subsequent pieces by Yoreh De'ah (140; 142,1.10.15; 143,1.3.6; 146,14f.; 147,1.2.5; 148,1.5f.9.10; 150,1-3), which deal with the behavior of the Jews toward "idols" and "idolatrous houses", Christian religious pictures and statues, as well as crosses and churches together with Christian worship, are also intended; because in the middle of this context, Isserles (Yoreh De'ah 141,1 Hagah) mentions the Christian cross, and the "*Gabbaîm*, who collect contributions for the (houses of) idols" are quite obviously Christian collectors, since we have not the slightest news about pagan collectors of a similar kind.

[6] Although this point is denied in the *Gemara* below.

> so she is helping to give birth to a child for idolatry. Nor may a Gentile woman be allowed to assist a Jewess in childbirth because they are suspected of bloodshed [the Gentiles against the Jews]—so says Rabbi Meîr. Authoritative scholars, however, say: one may let a Gentile woman assist a Jewess in childbirth if other Jews are standing by, but not if they [the Jewess and the non-Jewish midwife] are alone. ...Our rabbis have handed down: A Jewess may not suckle the child of a Gentile because she is thereby raising a child for idolatry."

There then follows an extensive discussion of Rabbi Meir's view that a Gentile woman may not suckle a Jewish child because she might put poison on her nipples and thus kill the Jewish child. And further, whether a Jewess should give birth to the Gentile only in return for payment, even on the Sabbath, or what reasons she might have to do so; likewise, the suckling of a Gentile child. The permission to suckle a non-Jewish child only in the event that an abundance of milk that causes the Jewess pain, dates only from post-Talmudic times.

Although already in the Book of Exodus, Jewish professional midwives in "Egypt" are presupposed, the Talmud apparently thinks primarily of married Jewish women and Gentiles who help a neighbor or friend of a different faith, or who help each other—and, in the case of the suckling women, who, perhaps as a result of the death of their child (or as a result of excess milk), are feeding the child of a person of a different faith. Above all, the conditions of a village or a small town and the peaceful coexistence of Jews and non-Jews are required. In the background, and indeed in the prohibition on mutual midwifery and wet nursing in the *Shulchan Aruch*, are Talmudic suspicions, but they are not mentioned. Jewish midwives and wet nurses for non-Jewish women should hardly exist today; only Jewish doctors as midwives for Christian women, Christian midwives and midwives for Jewish women, and a lot of Christian wet-nurses for Jewish children—something disapproved by strict Judaism.

Yoreh De'ah 158,2

> "The heretics, and those who practice idol worship [literally: worship of the stars], or who do sins for the sake of provocation, even one who ate forbidden foods or wore *shatnez* in order to provoke, this person is a heretic; and those who do not believe in the Torah and in the Jewish prophecy, it is commanded to kill them. If one has strength in his hand to kill them with a sword, in public, he should kill him".[7]

Yoreh De'ah 159,1

> "According to the wording of the Torah, it is permissible to lend to a non-Jew at interest [without mentioning the rate of interest]. But the rabbinical scholars have forbidden taking more interest than the lender needs for subsistence. But nowadays, it is permitted in every way, without restriction on the rate of interest."

Commentary: Deuteronomy 23:19f. (literally): "Thou shalt not take advantage of your [Israelite] brother with anything; but you may profiteer on the non-Jew." That the rabbis meant *real usury* is shown by the comment by the Bible and Talmud commentator Rashi on the (parallel) passage in Exodus 23:19: "Usury is like the bite of a snake [which first you hardly notice, but then it endangers life]. So at first, one also does not notice the usury, until it increases and [through compound interest, etc.] destroys a large fortune."

Since the Hebrew *thaschîch*, translated above as "may profiteer", can mean both "you *may*" as well as "you *should*," the great Maimonides, for example, understood the verse as a strict commandment:

> "The 198th commandment [of the Old Testament] is that God has commanded us to demand usury from the non-Jew (goy) and to lend to him only on this condition, so that we

---

[7] Ed.: Referenced by Bischoff but not included in the original book.

(in the lending) do not [really] benefit and help him, but rather harm him instead. Thus the holy Blessed One [God] holds: 'You shall take advantage of strangers.' On Psalms 75:5, David Kimchi (died 1232), as well as Isaac Abrabanél (died 1508) and others, translated *Lenochri thaschîch*: 'You can [may] take advantage of the non-Jew'."

Yoreh De'ah 232,12-14

"Anyone who is forced to swear an oath, his oath is void, even if he says that he is swearing according to the opinion of the majority and according to the opinion of God".

"If a Jew is coerced to make an oath or swear a vow, this is not an oath nor a vow...but is done only in order that one may be released from the coercion. ...It is [even] permitted to make such oaths or vows unsolicited and of one's free will, or to a greater extent than is required, ... because all this is done only out of compulsion... [B]ut let everything be done only insofar as it is necessary."

Hagah: "If a king or prince orders a Jew to testify under oath regarding another Jew, whether he has engaged in sexual intercourse with a non-Jew — in order to punish that Jew with death, this is called a 'compulsory oath', and this is to be invalidated internally. The same holds if (Jew) A has deposited money with (Jew) B and the king or prince orders that anyone who knows anything about A's money is to be banished. Such a ban, insofar as the Gentile ruler wants to take A's money by force unjustly, is completely null and void. And so B, with whom the money is deposited, may swear falsely that he has nothing from A, if only such people [as B] declare the oath invalid in their hearts and there is no profanation of the Name involved".[8]

[8] That is, no possibility exists that the perjury will be discovered and thus no disgrace will come upon God and the Jewish people.

> *Hagah*: "All this applies only if it is possible for one to make his oath falsely without the non-Jew knowing; otherwise it is forbidden 'because of the desecration of the Name'."

Yoreh De'ah 239, 1 (Hagah) – a perjury paragraph.

> *Hagah*: "If a Jew has stolen from a non-Jew, and the court makes him swear an oath in the presence of other Jews, and they know that he will swear falsely, they shall compel him to make a settlement with the (dispossessed) non-Jew and [exert an influence on him] *not* to swear falsely, even if he were [still] forced to take the oath, because his [obviously false] oath would desecrate the Name (of God).[9] If, however, he is forced to take an oath without there being a profanation of the Name in the matter [because no one can prove that he perjured himself], he should [swear falsely, but at the same time] destroy the oath in his heart [declare it invalid], because he was forced into it, as said above (Yoreh De'ah 232)."

The commentary *Beér ha-golah* remarks on this: "See there (923:14 *Hagah*): 'Where there is a risk of capital punishment, it is called an 'emergency oath' [if one perjures himself] and it doesn't matter whether the Name has been desecrated.' But in money-lawsuits, Isserles writes, perjury is allowed only if there is no desecration of the Name".

<u>Commentary</u>: Scarcely a word need be said about the fact that the "purely intellectual reservation" (*Reservatio pure mentalis*) is, in the case of a factually false oath, in equal measure legally and ethically punishable and reprehensible. Yoreh De'ah 239,1 itself not only speaks of the threat of the death penalty, but quite generally of a false (so-called) "purification"-oath of the accused. Even Yoreh De'ah 232,14 does not speak of capital punishment in the case of A, but of allegedly unlawful violence

[9] "Profaning the Name (of God)" in rabbinic parlance is the same as "bringing a bad name on the Jews and their God", if the forbidden action occurs.

by the ruler; whether such is present is left to the subjective judgment of B![10] Thus the concept of compulsion is given an inadmissibly wide scope, and in fact, for example, the strict Eastern Jew already feels "compelled" whenever he must swear an oath before a non-Jewish judge.

To make matters worse, all of these "purely intellectual reservations" about oaths, pledges, or sworn vows are only permitted here *in relation to non-Jews*. It is a misleading statement, and contrary to objective truth, when Hoffman claims, "in Yoreh De'ah 232,12-16, it is absolutely decided that all vows and oaths coerced by unjust threats are invalid, no matter whether they are extorted from [*read*: by] Jews or Christians (!), and whether or not a Jew or Christian, by failure to observe (!) the oath [*read*: by perjury!], is harmed." In the very next sentence, he must confess that in all places he only speaks of perjury *against a non-Jew*. He tries to get himself out of this jam by the dodge that the sources are at fault, namely the Responses (rabbinical legal opinions) etc.; and yet, in all these cases, the one deceived by the perjury was a "goy" (non-Jew) every time.

Strange! The *Shulchan Aruch* still knows very well how to draw a general rule from a special Responsum or a special case reported in the Talmud. It also knows, for example, how to distill the general prohibition of a mere "excitation of error" from plain fraudulent cases from the Talmudic source!

And why does the *Shulchan Aruch* (Choshen Mishpat 67,20) know how to provide such an excellent means for *Jewish judges* to know how to protect themselves and the "Jewish race" against perjury by a Jew *before a Jewish court?* Here, every private reservation is carefully ruled out (Choshen Mishpat 87,20 Hagah) with the admonition: "We do not let you swear according to your opinion, but according to *our* opinion."

In the face of this "compulsion" to tell the truth, which emanates only from the Jewish side, why is the Jew not allowed to "inwardly invalidate" his oath and, for example, with the assurance that he is swearing

---

[10] Thus, as the unquestioning apologist Fiebig himself explains, the justified claim of a non-Jew for the restitution of stolen property, as well as its justified recovery by non-Jewish courts, is regarded by the Jews as "coercion," and as "violent, groundless extortion", therefore as a compulsion—even though this is completely justifiable! Would the Jew also be entitled to a false oath, for example, against this "use of force"?

"according to the true meaning of the word and according to the opinion of God" (who forbids perjury), not swear perjury after all? Because he is dealing here with Jews and not with non-Jews!

— 6 —
TRANSLATIONS (3): CHOSHEN MISHPAT

Preliminary remarks. The polemic passages cited from the Choshen Mishpat have, to some extent, been interpreted more severely than they deserve; but on the other hand, however, an unsuccessful attempt has been made to clear them of guilt. In the case of David Hoffmann and other Jewish apologists of a lesser rank, that is understandable, especially since they represent an orthodox standpoint and the *Shulchan Aruch* is their guide in doctrine and life. This motive does not apply to Mr. Paul Fiebig; nevertheless, he never misses an opportunity to open himself up as an unconditional apologist of even dubious Jewish doctrines and customs! Apparently he owes the necessary apologetic tricks and 'whistles' in his work *Jews and Non-Jews* to the Kohan described in the foreword to *Rabbi and Deacon*. "Without this help," admits Fiebig himself, "I would not have been able to offer what I am offering as it is now." Only a semi-educated Lithuanian Jew, like that Kohan, who was otherwise very dubious, could also come up with similar tricks and prompt his gullible "pupil" Fiebig with such wisdom.

1. The first 'whistle' in the effort to immunize an embarrassing passage in the *Shulchan Aruch*, and especially its section Choshen Mishpat, is the assertion that the passage is to be understood as "time-historical." Therefore, it already existed in Karo's and Isserles' time and no longer had the meaning of its Talmudic original source, and especially not anymore today; only out of reverence and conservatism, has it been included in the *Shulchan Aruch*, but it is no longer valid! First of all, neither Karo nor Isserles wanted to create a collection of Talmudic relics of obsolete and no longer applicable regulations in the *Shulchan Aruch*, but instead, each of them, writes Fiebig, "wanted to present the current (!) law in order to provide the rabbis of his (!) time with a valuable aid for legal decisions".

In contrast to Maimonides, who also included regulations in his ritual and legal code *Yad Chasakah* which could only be valid again in the soon hoped-for messianic time, the *Shulchan Aruch* only wants to deliver, for this and every later time, practical and achievable regulations; it applies the Old Testament and Talmudic commandments in the sense of its time, but not in their "time-historical" original meaning. What is said there of "slaves" is considered by him as referring to "servants"; the Talmudic "Epicureans" are Jewish freethinkers of all colors from the 16th century and all that followed, because the Jewish doctrine should be applicable for all times (Talmud: "In the holy teaching, there is no earlier or later"). What is happening here today, as a result of changed times and accordingly changed customs has fallen out of practice, can regain validity or still applies elsewhere today, just as Rabbinic jurisdiction with purely Jewish courts of law applied and applies to many Eastern Jewish countries and others.

2. The second 'whistle' is to declare an uncomfortable passage in the *Shulchan Aruch* to be considered "purely legally". Fiebig, who has no idea of jurisprudence, lets Kahan, who is even less knowledgeable about it, prompt him to this as well as so many other things, and then says, with a solicitous glance to the side: "Lawyers will understand that. There is purely legal thinking that disregards everything moral".

Unfortunately, in my *Rabbinical Fables*, I cite two such cases of 'purely juridical thinking" in the Imperial Court, which hardly want to go into the morality of common sense. But that is not the issue here at all, only an apologetic trick! The *Shulchan Aruch* does not intend to engage in "purely legal thinking" or to offer gray legal theory, but, as Karo expressly says in his preface and Fiebig also emphasizes, to be a practical handbook of the applicable law for contemporary rabbis with their legal decisions, "a kind of mnemonic" that is far removed from all theorizing by nature! Truly! The *Shulchan Aruch*, which decides, with moral impartiality on the basis of its Rabbinical model, that two Jews, who together have swindled a non-Jew, should share the profits of the fraud (see below, Choshen Mishpat 183,7. Hagah), etc., acts far more honestly, and to that extent more morally, than this kind of apologist who calls the evaluation of such passages according to the clear wording "mechanical"; he creates the bad impression that such regulations seek to "excuse the bad impression of such regulations on unbiased people with inwardly untrue assertions and to turn everything around for the best. In the case of ethnic Jews (be they strict believers like Hoffmann or apostates like Kahan), one will at least be able to understand this; as for Fiebig's "genuine German science", I must confess my lack of scientific understanding.

3. The third 'whistle' is the assertion that the harshness of some "purely legal" provisions of the *Shulchan Aruch* are compensated for by the recommending of a milder procedure against non-Jews "for the sake of peace", "for the prevention of (non-Jewish) enmity" and out of consideration for the "profanation of the Name" (which is the "worst sin"), and that these formulas have been interpreted in a homiletic, educational sense and not in their simple, and really intended, legal meaning!

Marx-Dahlman rightly clarified that, for Karo in the *Shulchan Aruch*, "for the sake of peace" simply has the same meaning as "to avoid non-Jewish enmity", thus, despite the displeasure of some apologists, approximately means: "for the sake of a dear peace". And "profanation of the Name" means "juridically" nothing more than "an act which, if it comes out,[1] brings dishonor to the Jews and their God (among the non-Jews)".

To misinterpret these formulas in the "legally thinking" *Shulchan Aruch* in its favor as 'religiously edifying' is just as much a piece of artful deception as if someone wanted to derive from the legal concept of "good faith" in the Civil Code, the assertion that the Civil Code wanted to educate to "genuine German loyalty" and "ensure that the religion remains for the people!" The whole talk is put to an end by the equally true and courageous words of the thoroughly Jew-friendly, but objective Marx-Dahlman:

> "The motive for consideration is the peaceful relationship with the heathens [non-Jews], as long as the correlate is [only] the prevention of hatred, and the consideration itself is regarded as only an emergency required by the contemporary situation of the Jews, morally without value.... If it is justified to judge the morality of a religion according to the motives that have made it into the driving force of trade, then

---

[1] Marx-Dalman, very correctly: "If there is a risk that the inhuman act will become known."

the 'international or interdenominational morality of the old Rabbinism...must be assigned a very low level'."

*****

Choshen Mishpat 26,1

> "It is forbidden to litigate before the judges and in the court houses of the non-Jews, even if the non-Jewish judges judge according to Jewish law. Even if both Jewish parties agree to litigate before the non-Jewish judges, it is forbidden. But whoever does so is a miscreant and is as if he went out with contempt, blasphemy, and a raised hand against the law of our master Moses."

Fiebig "thinks here involuntarily of 1 Corinthians 1-6, where Paul forbids the Christians to litigate before the pagan courts." This is mere sand in the eyes. Paul is thinking of the inferior members of the Corinthian local community who, despite their unbelief, etc., are "appointed" as arbitrators by disputing members of the congregation. Fiebig's comparison with a German who would face a French, English, or Russian court is completely askew. Two Germans, e.g. in Paris, bring their legal dispute before French judges without further ado, without feeling like a "miscreant" and a despiser of the Civil Code! Even today, old school Jews would rather come to a bad private settlement than bring their civil dispute before non-Jewish judges. Of course, many "German citizens of the Jewish faith" naturally think differently about case of criminal charges against non-Jews.

Choshen Mishpat 28,3-4

> "If a non-Jew has a claim against a Jew, and a Jew knows how to testify on behalf of the Gentile to the disadvantage of the [defendant] Jew as the only available witness, and if the Gentile calls him to testify in a place where, in monetary matters, non-Jewish law already sentences the debtor to payment on testimony of one witness: then it is forbid-

den for the Jew to testify on the non-Jew's behalf; but if he has done so, the Jew is put under ban.

But if the non-Jew named the Jew as a witness from the outset, it would be a desecration of the Name if he [this Jewish witness] did not testify in favor of the non-Jew. In that case, he may testify on behalf of the non-Jew. If a Jew has a claim (of money) against a non-Jew, which the non-Jew disputes, and there is a witness in favor of this non-Jew, he may appear as a witness in favor of the non-Jew, if this non-Jew has asked him to testify."

Commentary: Jewish law (Deut 19:15) requires two witnesses against one defendant, while one witness is sufficient in favor of (the exoneration) of a defendant. Because Jewish law does not want to know anything from an individual incriminating witness, according to the interpretation of the text, the Jew who appears as the only witness in favor of a non-Jew against a Jew—i.e. before a non-Jewish court, for which even one incriminating witness is sufficient—violates this Jewish law, and he is therefore banned.

According to Jewish law, one witness for the defense is sufficient, and any number of persons can join them without doing anything contrary to Jewish law. In the first case, the Jew remains unpunished if he is summoned as a witness by the non-Jewish trial court, i.e. if he is in a "predicament" according to the Jewish view. If he were to deny knowing favorable testimony, this could perhaps easily come out in the process, and there would be a "desecration of the Name", i.e. a nasty inconvenience for Judaism, given by saying something like: "A nice people and a nice God, whose people make such waves!"

The spiteful effect of this provision is, that for purely formal reasons, the *Shulchan Aruch* prevents an honest Jew from helping the rights of a non-Jew to triumph, and thereby knowingly harms the non-Jew.

Choshen Mishpat 156,5 Hagah

"If a Jew has a non-Jew as a permanent customer, there are places where it is judged that other Jews are forbidden to compete with that first Jew; there are, however, places

> where it is not so judged.[2] Indeed, some allow any other Jew to go to the non-Jew, to lend to him, to do business with him, to propitiate him by gifts or favors, and thereby from that first Jew to lure him away. This is because [the first Jew has no legal privilege over "his" non-Jew, but rather] 'the belongings of non-Jews are like unclaimed property, and everyone who comes to them first is entitled to them'. Some, however, 'forbid' this."

<u>Commentary</u>: A Jew has, to use Fiebig's phrase, taken a non-Jew into a 'long-term lease' for himself—whether through loans, advances, or other business advantages or, as is still the case today in Poland, etc., as a court Jew through diligent management, favors, etc.—and feels to have permanently monopolized him. Then another Jew recognizes the good business. He therefore coaxes the chosen non-Jew by offering or granting all kinds of advantages in order to steal him away from the first Jew and to seize him for himself. Why should the monetary benefits of this business relationship with the "Goy" [non-Jew] flow solely into the pockets of the first-named Jew? The latter did not acquire the non-Jew for himself by contract, but only, so to speak, through the purchase price of the favors, etc. But the *Shulchan Aruch* itself says (Choshen Mishpat 271,4[3]) that a Jew does not acquire something that belongs to a Gentile by paying a purchase price, but only by means of a formal contract; before this is executed, anyone can appropriate what previously belonged to the non-Jew,

---

[2] In the text of the *Shulchan aruch* there is the word *Màarûphja*, which has the strangest origins. Marx-Dalman ("Jewish Foreign Law", p. 17) derives it from the Arabic *mà'rûf* (acquaintance). Others want to combine it with the Hebrew *ôrep* (neck) and still understand *màarûphja* as "the exclusive right of exploitation of a non-Jew". Professor Dr. Siegfried Passarge offers in his new edition of Brafmann's *The Book of the Kahal* numerous examples of how the Jewish Kahal (the community authority) publicly auctions "the" *Màarûpha*—meaning: "the privilege to be exclusively allowed to exploit a certain Christian" among the church members, in return for payment!

[3] "If a gentile sells a field to a Jew and has received the purchase price for it, but has not [yet] delivered a written contract for it, so it is that the field, that no longer belongs to the gentile, but does not yet belong to the Jew, is like an ownerless property that anyone who comes to first can occupy and appropriate."

since it is for so long regarded as "ownerless property." In the present case, therefore, a second Jew can seize the non-Jew for himself!

So far everything would be relatively harmless. However, the "legal proverb" emerged from neither the "agrarian", nor from the "commercial" cases, nor from the Talmudic-agrarian basis (Bava Batra 54a), which also only deals with a special case (Hoffmann, p. 45f.), but we already encounter it in absolute terms, without reference to a special case, in the Talmud (Bava Kamma 38a): "Rabbi Abahu said: 'Because the Gentiles [the children of Noah] did not keep the seven commandments [allegedly given to them],... God allowed their money to the Jews'." And the famous Talmud teacher Rashi comments on the story told on the same page about the Talmudic inequality of rights: "The rabbis did not reveal to them [the alleged Roman examiners of their laws] the true reason for this statute because of its dangerousness, namely, that the money of a non-Jew (to be taken) is like the seizure of an abandoned property"! Compare this to the statement of the highly famous Talmudist Rabbi Simeon ben Jochai in the Midrash *Wajjikra rabba*: "God permitted the Jews to take their money [the non-Jews], as it is written in Deut 20:14: 'And you shall eat the spoils of your enemies'."!

Moreover, with regard to the "idolaters" at least, it also says in Joseph Albo's *Ikkarim* III 25: "The body [the life] of an idolater is lawful for the Jew; even so much more is his money." From Bava Kamma 38a and Rashi, it emerges that the axiom of the "free as a bird" quality of non-Jewish money is much older than its use in the *Shulchan Aruch* and of far more general importance than its use there. Moreover, from Rashi we learn that this previously mentioned doctrine is kept secret from the non-Jews and is considered dangerous by the Jews themselves! Such is the state of affairs!

Choshen Mishpat 176,12 Hagah.

> "If someone [Jew A] has employed his fellow tribesman [Jew B] on the condition that B should do business with A's money, but that whatever B 'finds' [any windfall profit] should belong to him (B). And if B collects from an [errant] non-Jew debts already paid, then this unfair extra profit belongs under the concept of 'found' and Jew A had

> no claim to it, since the promissory that had been paid for only had paper value. [Jew B], who returned that money to the non-Jew, is under no obligation to repay that amount to his fellow tribesman. From the outset, it is also permitted by the same token."

Commentary: The somewhat tricky situation is this: Jew A has employed a Jewish "young man" (B) who is to take care of A's financial transactions, with the proviso that all extra profits that B makes from these transactions should belong to B. Among other things, A hands B a promissory note from a non-Jew (C), the amount of which, as A knows, the non-Jew C has already paid, but—through stupidity or negligence—without A having returned the promissory note at that time. A says nothing about it to B, who then shows the promissory note to the non-Jew C, and the stupid fellow actually pays the debt *again* in return for the handing over of the note. According to rabbinic law, B could now keep this sum for himself, firstly as a "find" (extra profit) contractually guaranteed to him and secondly, because it is also permitted, according to Rabbinic law, to take advantage of a non-Jew's business error.

But now B finds out somehow that the promissory note had already been paid for at the time, and that stupid C had just not been given the sum back. B is not a Jew of the *Shulchan Aruch* type, but rather a decent person and gives C back the money that was wrongly paid. When his principle A finds out about this, he gets angry and demands compensation from B for the lost business profit, saying that B should have shared the "find" with him—namely, C's mistaken repeated payment, or at least at this time the promissory note should not be surrendered either.

However, our *Shulchan Aruch* ruling rejects these claims of A: The "find" (extra profit) is contractually guaranteed to B alone. But B had to return the promissory note to C and thereby did not damage A, since every paid promissory note in honest business dealings is still only paper.

Choshen Mishpat 176,12 Hagah wants to protect the Jewish employee against the unjustified claims of his principal A, who is characterized as a really bad guy. By the way though, this rule is very interesting because of the strange, persisting rabbinic view that an error (when buying, selling, paying, etc.) is equal to "a loss," and that what was lost by a non-Jew should *only* be returned to him if there is reason to fear that the misappropriation of a "find" could cause unpleasant effects. The concluding sentence of the Hagah means that the non-Jew can immediately be given back what he has mistakenly overpaid, *if* the error is discovered while paying, e.g. his money can be returned to him immediately.

Choshen Mishpat 176,12 (continuation)

> "If a partner in a business has stolen or robbed something, he must share the profit with his partner. But if he suffers damage, he must bear it alone."

What Hoffmann says about this is immensely characteristic of the nature of his apologetics:

> "The court only must decide between the two litigants. The moral sermon [!], when [?] one or the other or both [?] have done wrong, does not belong in the legal code, and the duties of the two partners towards the robbed do not come under the 'laws for companions' [where the above text is], but under the laws on theft."

But what kind of "severe punishment" for such thieves and robbers will there be? Mr. Hoffmann reassures us: "The biblical law and also the *Shulchan Aruch* know no other punishment for robbery and theft than payment" (or the restitution, *but no criminal punishment*—very convenient for Jewish thieves and robbers!). Furthermore, the *Shulchan Aruch* prescribes, (Choshen Mishpat 26,1) according to the Talmud: "Whoever robs another is not obligated to seek out the [original] owner to return the stolen goods, but the robber can keep it with him until the owner comes and takes what is his." One may well ask how a person robbed in the street at night is supposed to know the address of the robber! Again, Hoffmann has advice: "It is clear that as long as the robbed person does not come forward, the court has to decide only between the two thieves [?] who are suspected of the robbery." Hoffmann says too little; but that alone is enough to show how 'free of morals' the Rabbinic law of the *Shulchan Aruch* is in comparison to the actual law.

Choshen Mishpat 183,7

> "Should a Jew send a [Jewish] messenger to receive money from a non-Jew, but the non-Jew mistakenly gives too much to that messenger, all the excess belongs to that messenger."
>
> *Hagah*: "But only if the messenger notices the overpayment before he has given all the money to his employer. If he has not noticed, but has already handed over the whole amount to his employer, then the whole amount belongs to him."

Here, too, the error of the non-Jew is a legitimate "find", in the sense of the *Shulchan Aruch* (vernacular: "a windfall"), for one of the Jews. There is no question here of returning the wrongfully acquired property, since the Jew does not have to give back to a non-Jew what he has lost. Nor is there any mention of a "sanctification of the Name" (by giving it back) or of giving back "for the sake of peace" or rather "to prevent hostility."

It suffices to state that here the *Shulchan Aruch* has simply to decide, in the sense of our Civil Code, which of two Jews is entitled to a reprehensible, "unjust enrichment" according to Rabbinic law!

> *Hagah***:** "If a Jew is making a commercial deal with a non-Jew, and another Jew comes along and helps him to mislead the non-Jew as to the measure, weight, or number of the bargained items, thus they must divide the dishonest gain, regardless of whether the second helped the first in return for payment, or for free."

Here, too, the error of the non-Jew is considered a legitimate "find" for the Jews. When Hoffmann, Fiebig, etc., in order to excuse the undeniably highly immoral regulation, say that we are dealing here with purely legal concepts, that morality "belongs in another chapter", one will ask in vain which "chapter" it is in the *Shulchan Aruch* that condemns that immorality. I doubt that any other code in the world has made such a decision as the that above! All the apologist arguments do not make this evil position any cleaner.

Choshen Mishpat 183,8

> "The Jew Ruben sends the Jew Simon, to buy him a robe from a non-Jew on credit. When the payment date comes, Ruben gives Simon the money to pay. Then it turns out that the non-Jewish seller himself cannot remember the business transaction at the time, and does not take the money. Simon then must give Ruben the amount back, and is not allowed to say: 'I want it with me, since the non-Jew might remember it' [namely, the business, and then want the money]. Likewise, he must not say, 'I will sanctify the Name and deliver it to the Gentile'!"

Choshen Mishpat 259,1 and 266,1

> 259,1: "Whoever sees a thing that a Jew has lost is obligated to make the effort to bring it back to him; for it says[4], 'you shall restore it to your brother'!"

> 266,1: "Keeping the lost property of a non-Jew is rabbinically lawful, for it says[5]: 'regarding your brother's loss.' But if the Jewish finder nevertheless returns the loss to the non-Jewish loser, he commits a violation of the law because he strengthens the [economic] power of the non-Jewish violators of the law. If, however, he brings it back to 'sanctify the Name', so that the non-Jews praise the Jews and recognize them as honest people, that is a laudable act."

<u>Commentary</u>: Both regulations are taken from the Talmud (Bava Metzia 26b or Bava Kamma 113b). When in our passage, Justus and Ecker say "grave" or "great sin" instead of violation the law, they simply want to render the Hebrew double expression *obêr abirâh* ('sinning by violating') quite correctly. That the *Shulchan Aruch sees something so bad in honesty toward a non-Jewish victim* makes the prescript hateful.

---

[4] Deut 22:1.

[5] Again, Deut 22:1.

Also it is incomprehensible why the *Shulchan Aruch* calls non-Jews "violators of the law"; Maimonides even calls them the "godless of the world"! Idolatry, fornication, etc. surely cannot, after all, be attributed to all of them! Joseph Karo says expressly in his *Beit Yosef*:

> "Here, all non-Jews are equally meant, whether idolatrous or not. And our rabbi was not accurate, if he meant only the idolaters. Perhaps he did that because in the land of Edom [Christian Europe], the baptized [Christianized] Jews suspected the believing Jews of the rulers of this and similar laws, whereupon the [Jewish] sages replied that only the [real] idolaters of the Talmudic era were meant."

This is how Karo, already 365 years ago, uses irony against the Jewish apologists, mentioned by Hoffmann, up to our days!

In the Talmud (Bava Kamma 113b) one reads:

> "What a non-Jew has lost, is permitted (to be kept) … because it says (Deuteronomy 22:3): 'What your brother has lost [you as the finder are to give it back]. You must give it back to your [Jewish] brother,' but not to a non-Jew. … However: Wherever there is the desecration of the Name (of God) [if, for example, the misdeed might become known], even what a non-Jew has lost may not be kept."

It is a general rabbinic axiom that the non-Jew is *not* the "brother" of the Jew. One sees that this rationale is decisive for keeping what the non-Jew has lost. Maimonides says instead: "…because it strengthens the power of the transgressors [non-Jews]"; and even more clearly: "…because he strengthens the power of the ungodly of the world [i.e. the ungodly non-Jews]"!

The famous Interpreter of the Bible, Raschi, also brings up a completely different reason than the Hoffmann-Fiebig "presupposition" to justify the Jewish misappropriation of finds regarding the non-Jew. He writes:

> "Whoever gives back to a non-Jew what was lost makes the non-Jew like a Jew [to whom what has been lost must be restored], and associates him with us Jews, and thereby proves in himself that he does not regard restoring [what was lost *only* to a Jew] as a commandment of his Maker, because he does the same with non-Jews—with regard to whom it is not commanded!"

Thus, the Jew, who returns lost property to the Gentile out of pure honesty—and not because the misappropriation might be exposed—really commits a "great sin" according to Rashi's opinion, because he allegedly disregards a divine commandment that commands giving back *only* to the "brother" Jew!

Incidentally, as is sometimes the case, Fiebig slaps himself in the face by citing the legal opinion of Rabbi Isaak bar Schescheth, in which it says, among other things: A Jew who informs a non-Jew that his Jewish debtor wants to flee in order to avoid paying the non-Jew, and thus protects the non-Jew from losing money, "has in any case done a great injustice, because he acted like one who brings back something lost to the non-Jew!"

Choshen Mishpat 283 Hagah

> "If a Jew owes a non-Jew, but the non-Jew has died and no non-Jew knows anything about the debt, he is not obligated to pay the debt to the heirs."

The principle that prevails throughout Rabbinism is this: "Whatever is not (in Jewish law) forbidden, is permitted," with all its highly wicked implications. And on the other side: "Whatever one is not expressly commanded to do (in Jewish law), one is not required do." This is not, as Fiebig says, "keen Jewish legal judgment", but a hair-splitting delivery service for unfair purposes! Because, for example, there is no commandment in the Old Testament that one should pay one's debts, so Rabbinism concludes from this that one need not do this at all if it is not noticed and no unpleasant consequences arise.

In passages below, this is applied almost as an axiom. A few isolated, irrelevant "sentimental words" praise it when a Jew returns a loan (Talmud, Ketubot 36a and Arakhin 22a); according to the Talmud and the *Shulchan Aruch*, however, the Jew does not need to do it—especially in relation to non-Jews—as long as he does not feel compelled to do so. Naturally the opinion also prevails elsewhere among noble souls: "Whoever pays his debts is wasting his fortune." Yet Fiebig, who again talks so gratuitously about "pure legality" etc., should show us another code of laws in the world, which says in plain words that one does not need to return money that has been borrowed—especially from people of other faiths!

Choshen Mishpat 348,2 and Hagah

> "Any Jew who steals, be it worth even a penny, violates the commandment (Lev 19:11): 'Thou shall not steal' and is obligated to return it; it doesn't matter whether he has stolen the money from a Jew or a non-Jew, an adult or a child."
>
> *Hagah*: "To take advantage of the error of a non-Jew is permitted, e.g. to let him err in arithmetic or by not paying off a loan that he forgot, [forgotten by him], provided he does not know it, so that no 'desecration of the Name' occurs. But some say it is forbidden to intentionally mislead the non-Jew; the exploitation of this error is only permitted if he has made a mistake of his own accord."

Commentary: This regulation is taken almost verbatim from Maimonides' Mishnah Torah, *Hilchôth genëbah* 1. In the Talmudic foundation, there is again talk of naked fraud. The paragraph reads:

> "Samuel said: 'The non-Jew's error is permitted for exploitation.' So Samuel [himself] bought a golden basin from a non-Jew [which the latter] took for a bronze one, for 4 dinars, and also shorted him by one dinar. Rab Kahana also bought 120 barrels from a non-Jew, instead of 100 and also cheated him, also by one dinar. He said to the non-Jew: 'See, I trust that you counted correctly.' Rabina bought

palm wood from a non-Jew; when the non-Jew was away, Rabina said to his servant: 'Go and chop off some of the thick end of the logs; for the non-Jew only knows the number' [but not the length].[6]

Here we have three deceptions. In the first of the three cases, the unsuspecting non-Jew offers the director of the academy, Samuel, a golden basin that is assumed to be made out of bronze. The rector, with "keen Jewish judgment," recognizes the true situation, but does not enlighten the non-Jew. Instead, he only pays as much for the basin as if it were really made of bronze; and on top of that, he knowingly cheats the inattentive non-Jew out of one dinar! What is that but double cheating?

In the second case, Rab Kahana notices that the non-Jew made a mistake in counting the number of barrels, and instead of 100 he offers him 120 barrels for sale. He says hypocritically: "I'm relying on you", and only pays him the price of 100 barrels for the 120 barrels; and on top of that, he cheats the absent-minded one by counting the purchase price from one dinar, so that the stupid non-Jew gets 3 dinars instead of 4.

Third, Rabina cheats (one may say: steals from) his non-Jewish business partner, who has only noted the number of logs they have purchased together, by secretly having his servant chop off some of the volume of the wood for himself.

According to our legal concepts, this would not only be "unjust enrichment", but also obvious fraud and, in the latter case, even theft. According to the Jewish view, however, wherever the non-Jew errs and allows himself to be deceived, this is a "find" for the enterprising Jew—a windfall—and anything thus "lost" by the non-Jew may be taken into possession by the Jew!

That was a little too strong for the medieval rabbis, and they allowed only the more subtle deception of the error by a non-Jew, by interpreting the expression *heteîth* ('to *make* err') as "to *let* err". So the famous French Rabbi Moses von Coucy said in his *Big Book of Laws*:

"The error of a non-Jew is permitted, if he has erred of his own accord. How so? If the non-Jew miscalculates to his

[6] See Appendix A.

> own detriment, the Jew says to him: "Look, I'm depending on your reckoning, I don't know, but I'll give you what you have said!" However, to *make* someone err is forbidden; for perhaps the Gentile miscalculates intentionally in order to set a snare for the Jew, whereby his deceitful intention would be revealed and the Name of heaven would be profaned."

In general, Maimonides and, following him, our *Shulchan Aruch* passage (in the Hagah) also says this.

The above Hagah (of Isserles) has always been very unpleasant for the Jewish and Judaizing apologists. This is true, even if such a gross or finer fraud occurs a thousand times in the life of "active business people." The awkward part is and remains that such things are in the *Shulchan Aruch*, which, after all, wants to present the applicable Jewish law and codify it in plain words!

The fortunately unnamed apologist author of the leaflet "Truths about Anti-Semitism" has the precious audacity to claim that the phrase from the *Shulchan Aruch*—"The error of a non-Jew is permitted, e.g. to let him err in counting"—was caused by a *typographical error* of a scribe, which was proven centuries ago by the relevant authorities. Of course, not a word of this is true. *"Audacity helps, even in relation to God"* is an old rabbinic sentiment[7]; but the brazen misleading of unsuspecting persons of the court and other Central Europeans is finally exposed after all!

Choshen Mishpat 369,6 and Hagah.

> "If a Jew is the tax collector for the king, a Jew who evades the tax robs the Jewish leaseholder. If, however, a non-Jew is the tax collector, then evasion is permitted, because it is then the same as not paying one's debt, which is [indeed] permitted in a case where no 'desecration of the Name' takes place."
>
> *Hagah*: "Some say that even if the tax collector is a Jew, and collects not for himself but for the king, the Jewish

[7] Sanhedrin 105a.

collector cannot force a Jewish evader to pay tax, even though evasion is forbidden by state law. This is because, here too, evasion is like not paying one's debt, which is allowed. But if there is reason to fear the king, then he can undoubtedly compel payment."

Commentary: The long and the short of it is this: The Jew may not cheat another Jew, but he may defraud a non-Jewish tax collector and even a non-Jewish ruler—and he may do so even if the national law forbids this.[8] The Jewish tax official and the Jewish tax-cheat are allowed to disregard the state law, if there is no danger of their damaging the non-Jewish state finances.[9]

According to Rabbinic Law, any monetary or similar damage to a co-religionist Jew is a punishable offense for the Jew. On the other hand, as we saw, it is permitted to do such damage to the non-Jew—provided that he does not notice it or cannot notice it. It is also permitted to evade customs duties or taxes to the detriment of the non-Jewish monopoly tenant or even the Gentile head of state. Yes, the Jewish tax collector, who does not work for his own purse, but who is entrusted with the collection of customs duties and taxes for the head of state and the state finances,

---

[8] Ed.: One can only imagine the degree to which wealthy Jews today employ such reasoning, to evade millions in taxes.

[9] In the Middle Ages, respected Jews were not only treasurers, chief treasurers, and general treasurers of the Kings, but also tax collectors on their own account or customs collectors on behalf of the government. They acted so "successfully", especially at the expense of the Christian population, that they became massively rich people—even receiving an honorary salary from the state! The baptized Jews Luis de Santangel and Gabriel Sanchez made possible the first voyage of discovery of Columbus in January 1492 [who was himself likely Jewish (Ed.)]. Isaak Abrabanél (1437-1508), the famous Jewish interpreter of the Bible, was in turn the finance minister for Alfonso IV of Portugal, for Ferdinand of Aragon and Isabella of Castile (from 1484), and for Ferdinand I of Naples and his successor Alfonso II (from 1492). In 1492 he offered Ferdinand of Aragon, who was always in need of money, a huge sum if he would not drive the Jews out of Spain (to no avail); with crucifix in hand, he implored Peter von Arbues, since 1485 Judge of the Inquisition, not to betray Jesus again for Jewish pieces of silver. Incidentally, Thomas de Torquemada, the Spanish Grand Inquisitor from 1483, was himself a Jew.

should not even stand in the way of his co-religionists during these intrigues, as long as there is no danger of the exposure of this consensual racketeering!

In further discussing, whether such undercutting against a non-Jew is not "robbery," Raba (Bava Kamma 113b) explains that it is, in fact, simply "not paying a debt"—which is permitted.[10]

The key point of the question, namely that the Jew may cheat a non-Jewish tax tenant through evading customs and taxes, Hoffmann cheerfully omits, according to the well-known rabbinical trick of talking past the matter when embarrassed!

Incidentally, our passage is especially interesting because of the intrinsically revealing position of the rabbis on the much-discussed sentence: *State law is (also) law.*[11] With the exception of the corruption of the religious-instructional meaning of the expressions "Sanctification, or rather, desecration of the Name" and "for the sake of peace," which were "purely legally" thought out and applied in the *Shulchan Aruch*, no rabbinic expression from the Jewish and half-Jewish apologists is as brazenly abused as this one. This sentence was not lacking in almost any rabbinical meeting as 'proof' of the state and civil loyalty of Judaism—alongside the assurance that, today, the non-Jew is also considered a "brother" to the Jew. And it was then exploited apologetically, as if it were "a statue of Moses from Sinai". Even Hoffmann, who knows the true facts, says obliquely: "Law of the state government is (valid) law", although he could at most say: "valid law, under certain circumstances".

The Weimar state rabbi, who was publicly rebuked in my *Rabbinical Fables*, probably reaches the peak of irresponsibility when he falsified Samuel's sentence: "The principle applies everywhere: State law is religious law."(!) And this "nonsense on horseback" in connection with the possibly even more unbelievable leaflets of the "Central Association of German Citizens of the Jewish Faith" were presented to a German court as the honest truth! In my *Rabbinical Fables*, I have also cleared out this nasty corner of the apologetic-polemical Augean stable and have concisely proven to the imprudent Mr. State Rabbi, that both in the

---

[10] "The direct robbery of the non-Jews is forbidden, but one does not have to pay him a debt, and customs duties are also considered as such" (according to Goldschmidt).

[11] Ed.: In other words, civil law is also a 'law,' along with 'Jewish law.'

Talmudic source (Bava Kamma 133a) and everywhere in the Rabbinical Literature, the uncomfortable sentence of Samuel applies, that state law (in certain cases) also applies, but never goes unchallenged, and is always subject to significant restrictions or declared inapplicable, as for example, in the matrimonial cases dealt with in the *Shulchan Aruch* (Choshen Mishpat 369,11 Hagah), where it says openly: "In this case it does not apply: 'State law [is law]'..."—because otherwise all Jewish law would be abolished.[12] And Hoffmann himself has to admit: "However, this principle of Samuel generally conceived and consistently implemented, would have eliminated Jewish law and put state law in its place." With this, the posturing of the apologists and defenders is, once and for all, put to an end. Samuel simply wanted to know, when the Sassanids demanded that all inhabitants of the country follow the laws of the country, whether they were allowed to obey non-Jewish laws in civil law, and explained to them that these laws were also binding—*as long as they did not contradict Jewish laws.*[13]

Far higher than Samuel's mere adaptive morality are Paul's words: "Everyone is subject to the government that has power over him", with the religious justification: "For there is no government but God" etc.[14] And even higher, Jesus' words (also a tax question): "Render to Caesar what is due to Caesar, and to God what is due to God" (Matt 22:21). Perhaps the question that we should put to Pastor Paul Feibig is whether or where Jesus said, for example, that if the tax payer or the tax collector was a non-Jew, one did not have to give the emperor the money due to him.

---

[12] Ed.: The final sentence of 369,11 reads, "The principle of government law does not apply here because we do not say the principle except for something where there is a benefit to the king or it is a regulation for the citizens, but not that they litigate in secular court, because if that were to happen, all Jewish laws would become void."

[13] Ed.: In other words, respect both laws, but when push comes to shove, Jewish law trumps civil law.

[14] Ed.: As we read in Romans 13:1: "Let every soul be subject to the governing authorities. For there is no authority except by God; and those existing have been instituted by God."

Choshen Mishpat 388,10 and Hagah 388,15

> "Even today it is lawful in any place to kill the informer. But it is only permitted to kill him *before* he has carried out the denunciation. In fact, when he says: 'Behold, I will denounce so-and-so in body or money', even if it is only a little money, at that moment, he has given himself up to death of his own accord. And he should be warned and told: 'Don't denounce!' But if he defiantly says, 'No, I will denounce him after all,' then it is a commandment to kill him, and anyone whoever kills him first is in the right."
>
> *Hagah*: "But if there is no more time for warning, then it is not necessary. Some say that one should only kill the informer if one cannot save oneself from him by damaging one of his limbs. If this is possible, for example, by cutting out his tongue or blinding his eyes, it is forbidden then to kill him, because he is no worse than the rest of the persecutors."
>
> *Hagah*: "If a Jew has been proven to hand over a Jew or their money into the hands of a Gentile three times, we would seek counsel and plans to have him removed from the world indirectly. ... Regarding the expenses incurred to get rid of the informer, all the inhabitants are obliged to contribute, even those who pay taxes in another place."

Commentary: 388,10 is taken from a ""haggadic" (narrative) report in the Talmud, which was only transformed into "halachic" (normative) by the rabbis. In Bava Kamma 117a, it says only briefly and edifyingly:

> Once someone wanted to denounce the [evaded] straw of another Jew. When he came before Rabh about it, the latter said: 'You shall not, you shall not report it!' The other responded: 'I will still do it, surely I will report it!' Then Rab Kahana, who was sitting in front of Rabh, got up and broke that informer's neck.[15]

---

[15] Arriving in Palestine, the murderer was not shunned, but honorably accepted into the circle of the disciples of the famous Rabbi Yochanan. A clear path for the brave!

The "Central Association of German Citizens of the Jewish Faith" has spread the nonsense in its leaflet, "Truths about Anti-Semitism" [read: "Jewish Lies"] that through some commissioned ignoramus, the informer intends or has already attempted to release slanderous denunciations against the Jews. Of course, the opposite is true: the informer wants to betray the tangible facts both in the Talmud and in the *Shulchan Aruch*, namely, the evasion of taxable Jewish supplies, which certain Jews want to cheat away, contrary to the stated precept "State law is the law"!

Oddly striking is the instruction to kill the informer before he denounces, whereupon it says: "If the denunciator has already carried out his intention, it is forbidden to kill him, unless he is known to betray yet further. For such a one is to be killed, so that he might not betray others". Despite somewhat confused wording and the intervening thirst for revenge and the blood of the denunciator, the facts are clear: to kill the informer *after* he has denounced would be very dangerous for the Jews; for the non-Jewish authority to which he has made his denunciation would hold the Jews heavily responsible if they wanted to kill the possible chief witness to the authority. *Before* the denunciation, however, and in the case of an admitted intention to denounce, the informer can be killed without danger, since the non-Jewish authorities do not know that or what he wanted to denounce. And in the worst case, one can declare the death "harmless", but justify it to one's own knowledge by saying that one acted in self-defense or supposed self-defense, which is also present when one wants to ward off an imminent danger from others.

The Jews still have sufficient means at hand against the denunciation that has taken already place: "If the [Jewish] informer has denounced the Jewish community and thus puts them in a difficult position," then one seeks, for example, by means of a counter-denunciation to the non-Jews, which is attested to as true by the Jewish majority, to somehow portray him as guilty and to pursue his punishment. For, "in such a case, it is permissible to hand him over to the Gentiles, to be beaten, to be imprisoned, and sentenced to punishment" (Choshen Mishpat 388,12). "Because of the bad situation of an individual Jew caused by the informer", this is not permitted. At first, one tries with all means to free the denounced Jewish brothers from the raised suspicion. But if this has happened three times, then one goes against the informer, in order to make it impossible for him to continue his activities by means of the fabricated "self-defense"—which can only be construed as the elimination of the informer by hired assassins. Within the context of the texts, I cannot imagine any other possibility to put an end, with certainty and forever, to an informer regarded as malicious and incorrigible.

Choshen Mishpat 406,1

> "If the ox of a Jew has kicked the ox of a non-Jew, he is free from blame. But if the ox of a non-Jew has kicked the ox of a Jew, he the non-Jew must pay all of the damages, whether or not his ox was known to be bucking."

This rule is an old famous one from the Talmud (Bava Kamma 38a). It is based on the Old Testament passage (Exodus 21:35), which regulates a case of damages between two Jews.[16] The Talmud concluded: The Bible passage refers only to the ox killed by "the neighbor"; according to the prevailing rabbinic view, however, *only another Jew* counts as a "neighbor", not the non-Jew. The case of his ox being killed by a non-Jewish ox does not occur at all in the Old Testament. As a result, the Jew here does not owe the non-Jew any damages, which he would owe the Jew. If the non-Jew, nevertheless, makes a claim for damages against the Jewish owner of the ox before a Jewish court, he will be dismissed outright, because "Moses does not write anything" about such a matter!

On the other hand, the injured Jew may demand full compensation from the non-Jew, whether before a Jewish or non-Jewish court. It is reminiscent of the already often-mentioned Talmud passage Bava Kamma 113a,21:

> "If you can make the Jew win according to Jewish law, do so, and say to the non-Jew: 'This is *our* law!' However, if you can make him win according to non-Jewish law, do so, and say to the non-Jew: 'This is *your* law!'"

---

[16] "If someone's ox hurts the ox of another, so that it dies, then they shall sell the live ox and divide the price of it, and the dead animal they shall also divide. But if it was known that the ox was accustomed to gore in the past and its owner did not restrain it, the owner shall restore ox for ox but keep the dead animal."

Now here is a case where the Jew wins according to both laws, and in both cases, the non-Jew is rejected with his claim.[17]

This "pearl in the mouths of the Rabbis" could therefore not be missed by the "codices", least of all the *Shulchan Aruch*, whose harsh attitude toward non-Jews as persons of inferior rights and also otherwise inferior people is clear, and which the commentators so often try to mitigate. One does not really see why this specific regulation was included in the medieval Jewish "codices", since apart from a few cattle dealers, a Jew as an ox owner was a very rare exception. Is this a prime example for the rejection of non-Jewish claims for damages, because the Old Testament grants the corresponding claims only to the Jew? Or was the decisive factor for its inclusion the fact that, here, the rabbinic principle comes to light in a particularly harsh way that the "neighbor" for the Jews according to the Old Testament text is *only the Jew*, but in no case is he a non-Jew?

---

[17] Ed.: There could hardly be a clearer statement of Jewish duplicity. Jews will apply any law, any rule, under any circumstance, simply to come out ahead.

APPENDIX A

Translations from the Talmud

Editor: As mentioned by Bischoff in chapter one, the Talmud as a whole is divided into six major units or divisions, each of which is called a *seder* (plural: *sedarim*). Each seder, in turn, is divided into several "tractates" or chapters, numbering between 7 and 12, depending on seder. Specific quotations—such as below—usually cite only the tractate and then the line number within the tractate; occasionally one will find the seder cited as well.

The seder/tractate structure is as follows:

Seder #1: *Zeraim* ('seeds')

Tractates:	Berakhot	Shevi'it	Challah
	Pe'ah	Terumot	Orlah
	Demai	Ma'aserot	Bikkurim
	Kil'ayim	Ma'aser Sheni	

Seder #2: *Moed* ('festival')

Tractates:	Shabbat	Yoma	Ta'anit
	Eruvin	Sukkah	Megillah
	Pesahim	Beitza	Mo'ed Katan
	Shekalim	Rosh Hashanah	Hagigah

Seder #3: *Nashim* ('women')

Tractates:	Yevamot	Sotah
	Ketubot	Gittin
	Nedarim	Kiddushin
	Nazir	

Seder #4: ***Nezikin*** ('damages')

Tractates:	Bava Kamma	Makkot	Avot
	Bava Metzia	Shevu'ot	Horayot
	Bava Batra	Eduyot	
	Sanhedrin	Avodah Zarah	

Seder #5: ***Kodashim*** ('holy things')

Tractates:	Zevachim	Arakhin	Tamid
	Menachot	Temurah	Middot
	Hullin	Keritot	Kinnim
	Bekhorot	Me'ilah	

Seder #6: ***Tohorot*** ('pure things')

Tractates:	Keilim	Tohorot	Zavim
	Oholot	Mikva'ot	Tevul Yom
	Nega'im	Niddah	Yadayim
	Parah	Makhshirin	Uktzim

The following passages have been taken, in modified form, from the website www.sefaria.org. The reader should note that there are a variety of spellings for certain of the tractates: 'Hullin' versus 'Chullin,' 'Beitza' versus 'Beitzah,' 'Hagigah' versus 'Chagigah,' etc. Note also that Sefaria lists some tractates under 'Babylonian Talmud' and others under 'Jerusalem Talmud.'

In addition to the above formal (canonical) tractates, there are another 14 so-called 'minor tractates' that are also recognized as Jewish law:

Avot D'Rabbi Natan	Kallah	Semachot
Avadim	Kallah Rabbati	Soferim
Derekh Eretz Rabbah	Kutim	Tefillin
Derekh Eretz Zuta	Mezuzah	Tzizit
Gerim	Sefer Torah	

All following text is direct from the Talmud, unless marked 'commentary'—which, along with the notes, are by Bischoff (unless otherwise specified).

*****

Bava Kamma ("The First Gate")

113a: One may vow before murderers, plunderers, and tax collectors in order to reinforce the claim that a certain item that is being commandeered is *Hebe*,[1] or that it belongs to the government, and thereby avoid its seizure, despite the fact that it is not *Hebe* or that it does not belong to the government. It was asked: Can it be that it is permitted to pronounce such a vow before tax collectors? But doesn't Samuel say: "The law of the state is the law!"? It should therefore be prohibited to state such a vow before the tax collectors.

Rabbi Ḥanina bar Kahana said that Samuel says: The Mishnah in *Nedarim* issues its ruling with regard to a tax collector who does not have a limitation placed on the amount he may collect. Alternatively, the Sages of the school of Rabbi Yannai say: The Mishnah issues its ruling with regard to a tax collector who stands on his own.

Rav Ashi said: The Mishnah issues its ruling with regard to a *Gentile* tax collector, whom one may deceive: In the case of a Jew and a Gentile who approach the court for judgment in a legal dispute, if you can vindicate the Jew under Jewish law, vindicate him, and say to the Gentile: *This is our law*. If he can be vindicated under Gentile law, vindicate him, and say to the Gentile: *This is your law*. And if it is not possible to vindicate him under either system of law, one approaches the case with *legal trickery*,[2] seeking a justification to vindicate the Jew. This is the statement of Rabbi Ishmael.

Rabbi Akiva disagrees and says: One does not approach the case with trickery in order to vindicate the Jew due to the sanctification of God's name, as God's name will be desecrated if the Jewish judge employs dishonest means.

And even according to Rabbi Akiva, the reason that the court does not employ trickery in order to vindicate the Jew is only because there is the consideration of the sanctification of God's name. Consequently, if

---

[1] Fruit from the fields or groves that is set aside for Jewish religious purposes.
[2] Goldschmidt uses the word "deceit" [other translations use 'circuitously'—Ed.]. The meaning is: The Jewish judge should confuse the non-Jew with all sorts of speeches and sophistry so that he refrains from his complaint or allows himself to be persuaded to pay the accused, etc. A truly judicial settlement is not allowed.

there is no consideration of the sanctification of God's name, the court does approach the case circuitously. Apparently, it is permitted to deceive a Gentile.

113b: It is permitted to retain the Gentile's lost item, as Rav Ḥama bar Gurya says that Rav says: "From where is it derived that it is permitted to retain the lost item of a Gentile? It is derived from a verse, as it is stated: 'With every lost thing of your brother's' (Deut 22:3), indicating that it is *only to your brother* that you return a lost item, *but you do not return a lost item to a Gentile.*" [...]

It is taught that Rabbi Pineḥas ben Ya'ir says: "In a case where there is a concern that retention of an article lost by a Gentile will result in the desecration of God's name, it is prohibited to retain even a Gentile's lost item."

Samuel says that *it is permitted to financially benefit from a business error of a Gentile*, i.e., it need not be returned. The Gemara notes that this is like that incident where Samuel purchased a golden bowl from a Gentile in exchange for the price of an iron bowl, which was four dinars, and Samuel included one additional dinar in the payment so that the Gentile would not realize his mistake.

The Gemara relates another incident: Rav Kahana purchased 120 barrels from a Gentile for the price of 100 barrels, and he included one additional dinar in the payment. Rav Kahana said to him: "Take note that I am relying upon you to check that the transaction has been carried out properly." The Gemara records a third episode: Ravina and a Gentile purchased a palm tree together in order to chop it up and split the wood between them. Ravina said to his attendant: "Hurry and precede the Gentile so that you can bring my share of the wood from the trunk of the tree, which is thicker than the upper part of the tree, as the Gentile knows only the number of logs that he is due to receive and will not realize that you are taking thicker pieces".[3]

---

[3] Although this statement is "haggadic", meaning it is narrative, Isserles used it in the *Shulchan Aruch* to compose his "Hagah", which has become so famous in polemics and apologetics: "The error of a non-Jew—e.g. making him err in arithmetic or not paying him a debt that he overlooks—is permissible, but only if he does not realize it, so that no 'desecration of the Name' takes place. Some say it is forbidden to cause him to blunder, and it is only permitted if he him-

Nedarim ("Oaths")

20b,4: However, the Rabbis said: The *halakha* is not in accordance with the opinion of Yoḥanan ben Dehavai. Rather, whatever a man wishes to do with his wife he may do. He may engage in sexual intercourse with her in any manner that he wishes, and need not concern himself with these restrictions. As an allegory, it is like meat that comes from the butcher. If he wants to eat it with salt, he may eat it that way. If he wants to eat it roasted, he may eat it roasted. If he wants to eat it cooked, he may eat it cooked. If he wants to eat it boiled, he may eat it boiled. And likewise with regard to fish that come from the fisherman.

A certain Jewess, who came before Rabbi Yehuda HaNasi to complain about her husband, said to him: "My teacher, I set him a table, using a euphemism to say that she lay before him during intimacy, and he turned it over." Rabbi Yehuda HaNasi said to her: "My daughter, the Torah permitted him to engage in sexual intercourse with you even in an atypical manner, and what can I do for you if he does so?"

Child Sexualization

1. Three-year-old Jewish Girls

Niddah ("Menstruating Women")

44b,9-12: A girl who is three years and one day old, whose father arranged her betrothal, can be married through intercourse. And in a case where the childless husband of a girl three years and one day old dies, if his brother [i.e. the brother-in-law] engages in intercourse with her, he acquires her as his wife. And if she is married, a man other than her husband is liable for engaging in intercourse with her due to violation of the prohibition against intercourse with a married woman.

---

self has made the mistake." Thus, there are still more often "haggadic" parts that have been incorporated into the Talmud, than halachic parts into the *Shulchan Aruch.* It is characteristic of rabbinic duplicity that the above-mentioned Samuel says on the one hand "state law is the law", and on the other hand, declares that the exploitation of an "error by the non-Jew" is permitted.

And if she is impure due to menstruation, she imparts impurity to one who engages in intercourse with her who then renders impure all the layers of bedding beneath him, rendering them impure…

If she marries a priest, she may eat from the *Hebe* like any other wife of a priest. If she is unmarried and one of the men who are unfit for the priesthood engaged in intercourse with her, he disqualifies her from marrying into the priesthood. Finally, if one of all those with whom relations are forbidden, as stated in the Torah, e.g., her father or her husband's father, engaged in intercourse with her, they are but to death by the court for engaging in intercourse with her; but she is exempt, because she is a minor.

<u>Commentary</u>: The same teaching, which has become a Talmudic axiom, is found among others: Yevamot 57b, 60b; Kiddushin 10a; Ketubot 9a (6b, 11b); and Niddah 64b.

This passage was very unpleasant for that great father of the Jews, Prof. Franz Delitzsch, as well as for his house Jews (Biesenthal, Kahan, etc.), who were supposed to say something apologetic regarding it, but only knew how to talk past the point. Thus, he referred to Löwe's *Lebensalter*, where nothing is written about it, and furthermore to the Mosaic-Talmudic prohibitions against pederasty(!), which have absolutely nothing to do with this, and to the equally unrelated Talmudic prohibition of employing unmarried teachers for children(!). And he ranted, not at the clear Talmudic passages about the above-mentioned child abuse, but at "Brudling's impure imagination and unbridled malice", that "lie about the Talmud with impunity"!

But all Jewish cover-ups and apologetic abuse is useless against the truth: the passages and even much worse ones (see below) are there, and they cannot be explained away or reinterpreted.[4]

---

[4] The famous Bible and Talmud interpreter Rashi (1040-1105) calculates from Genesis 25:20 that Isaac was 37 years old when Rebekah was born, and then continues: "Rebekah was born at this time, and after waiting three years until she was fit for intercourse, he took her (as his wife)." In a similar way, by means of a demented chronology in Sanhedrin 69b, it is calculated from Old Testament passages that Bathsheba gave birth to Solomon when she was six years old. She would have given birth to her deceased child by David (2 Samuel 12:15) when she was five at the latest, so that she could have committed adultery with David when she was four. But since she had already been the

Other “Christian experts”, however—like Professors Nöldecke and Wunsch—would ultimately not be able to find this or that well-known passage of the Talmud “at the given place”, although it is literally and clearly found in every copy of the Talmud available in the whole world(!). False translations do not garner any greater authority; and I, at least, have disciplined the Weimar National Rabbi Dr. Wiesen sufficiently for such a thoughtless treatment. Thus, as a last resort, it would probably only remain for them to falsify, without further ado, in future Talmud editions such “embarrassing” texts as those quoted in this section.

2. Even Younger Jewish Girls

Niddah 44b,12: If the [Jewish] girl is less than that age, younger than three years and one day, the status of intercourse with her is not that of intercourse in all halakhic senses; rather, it is like placing a finger into the eye. Just as in that case, the eye constricts, sheds tears, and then returns to its original state, so too, in a girl younger than three years and one day old, the hymen returns to its original state.

Commentary: As Lazarus Goldschmidt rightly points out, it is a Talmudic axiom that the stolen virginity of a little girl so violated could be restored, which of course is a physical impossibility.

There is probably no religious document in the world that allows such abominations as those just mentioned. Jewish and “Christian” apologists have objected that these are all “legal theories” drawn from misunderstood passages in the Bible without any factual background. It is an eternal pity that it is *the Talmud itself* that denounces these audacious sages of fraud! Yevamot 60b states in clear words:

> 60b,15: As Rabbi Yehoshua ben Levi said: There was a certain city in Israel where they contested the lineage of a particular family. And Rabbi Yehuda HaNasi sent Rabbi Romanus, and he examined the family’s lineage and found that it included the daughter of a convert who had convert-

---

wife of the Hittite Uriah for a while, he must have married her when she was only three years old!

> ed when she was less than three years and one day old, and she had married a priest. And Rabbi HaNasi declared her lawfully married.
>
> 60b,19: A certain priest married a convert, who had converted when she was less than three years and one day old. Rav Naḥman bar Yitzḥak said to him: "What is this? Why are you violating the *halakha*?" He said to him: "It is permitted for me to marry her…"

Meanwhile, the circumcised and uncircumcised apologists will say, with raised eyebrows and raised forefingers, that in cases 1 and 2 it is a little Jewess, after all, and furthermore that it is a "shameless lie", and who knows what else, to claim that in the Talmud even a little three-year-old Gentile girl is declared suitable for intercourse—but not for marriage, of course.

3. Three-year-old *Non*-Jewess

Avodah Zarah 37a,1: Ravina said: Therefore, regarding a female Gentile child who is three years and one day old, since she is fit to engage in intercourse at that age, she also imparts impurity like one who is menstruating.

4. Gentile Boys

Avodah Zarah 36b-37a: They decreed upon a male Gentile child that he imparts ritual impurity as though he were a Jew who experienced a vaginal discharge, so that a Jewish child will not become familiar with him, leading to homosexual intercourse. As Rabbi Zeira says: I had great torment with Rabbi Asi when I asked him… The inquiry was as follows: From when does a Gentile child impart ritual impurity like one who menstruates? From when he is nine years and one day old.

The Gemara explains the reason for this opinion: Since a nine-year-old boy is fit to engage in intercourse,[5] he also imparts ritual impurity as

---

[5] Sanhedrin 69b,6: "Rabbi Ḥiyya says that Rav Ḥisda says, and some say that Rav Ḥisda says that Ze'eiri says: All concede, regarding a boy nine years and one day old, that his intercourse is regarded as intercourse… And they also all

one who menstruates. Ravina said: Therefore, regarding a female Gentile child who is three years and one day old, since she is fit to engage in intercourse at that age, she also imparts impurity as one who menstruates.

The Gemara asks: Isn't that obvious? The Gemara explains: It was necessary to state this ruling, lest you say that the *halakha* that a Gentile who is suited for intercourse imparts impurity does not apply to a female. The possible difference between a male and female child is based on the fact that whereas that child, a nine-year-old male Gentile, knows how to accustom others to sin by employing persuasion, this child, a three-year-old female Gentile, does not know how to accustom others to sin until she matures. Therefore, Ravina teaches us that the *halakha* nevertheless applies to both male and female children.

Commentary: "Because he knows how to seduce," explains Goldschmidt correctly; "In a nine-year-old boy [according to the Talmudic view], the sex drive is already mature, but not in a three-year-old girl." This leads to the downright atrocious and appalling authorization of intercourse with small children! The little being is declared "suitable" for defilement (rape), even though it has yet no sexual drive, and in the horrible act it derives no pleasure—as is presupposed in the case of the nine-year-old boy—but suffers only pain! And worse still: the *Jewish* three-year-old acquires at least the full rights of a Jewish wife through the bestial act on the part of the Jew, while the *non-Jewish* three-year-old child has nothing but pain and shame, because according to religious law, the Jew is not allowed to marry his victim!

Certain apologists will have to "torment" themselves even more than Rabbi Zeira (mentioned above) in order to make "moral tales for

---

concede, concerning a boy less than eight-years-old, that his intercourse is *not* regarded as intercourse vis-à-vis these *halakhot*. They disagree only about a boy who is eight years old..."

And further, by means of subtle conclusions from Old Testament verses, it is verbosely "proven", that Haran (Abraham's brother) fathered Sarah (Abraham's future wife) when she was eight-years-old; it was the same with others. Before that there was a difference of opinion in the well-known schools of Shammai and Hillel, how to decide if a widow had committed sexual immorality with her son who was under 13 years of age—namely, whether or not she would then be able to marry a priest. And the question was answered in the affirmative!

such children" from the cited passages! As an aside: According to an indictment by the public prosecutor in Plauen, the preacher of the local Jewish community, Emanuel Heimann, swore as a witness before the Plauen Court "that the desecration of female persons, regardless of whether they are of Jewish descent of not, is an extremely serious sin, according to Israelite religious law." When he was supposed to appear before the criminal court as an expert and comment on the above-cited Talmud passages, he promptly declared himself to be biased as a Jew, and a mere "preacher" not sufficiently knowledgeable about the Talmud (!!!), whereupon the court dismissed him. I would have loved to teach him!

Although modern Jews like to boast about their "successes" with adult Gentile girls—of course, not "for the purpose of later marriage"—and although Jewish molesters of young Gentile children are often condemned, I am, of course, a long way from presenting such passages as the above as binding Talmudic statutes, according to which our German citizens of the Jewish faith have also acted. On the contrary, I am convinced that among the many thousands, hardly anyone at all has any idea about these passages. And if someday the Jewish molestation of small children of the kind mentioned should ever become known, I would at worst think: *This looks almost as if the Jewish criminal is unconsciously following the criminal reasoning of the old Talmud rabbis*. My sole concern is in communicating this and other Talmudic passages of Halachic content, merely to show to what lunacy rabbinical sophistry has degenerated.

Again, all this from the Talmud; the *Shulchan Aruch* is free from these bestial permissions![6]

Rabbinical Sophistry

Bava Metzia 114b,2: Rabbi Shimon ben Yoḥai says that the graves of Gentiles do not render one impure, as it is stated: "And you, my sheep, the sheep of my pasture, are man" (Ezekiel 34:31), which teaches that you, i.e., the Jewish people, are called "man," but Gentiles are not called "man."

---

[6] Ed.: But this fact, of course, does not mean that such permissions are not formal parts of Jewish law; as direct passages from the Talmud, they are indeed still recognized as law.

Keritot 6b, 19-20: One who applies the anointing oil to animals or vessels is exempt, and one who applies it to gentiles or to corpses is exempt. The Gemara objects: Granted, one is exempt in the case of animals and vessels, as it is written: "Upon the flesh of a person it shall not be applied" (Exodus 30:32), and animals and vessels are not the flesh of a person. It is also clear why one is exempt if he applies it to a corpse, as once someone has died, the body is called a corpse and not a person. But if one applies anointing oil to Gentiles, why is he exempt? Aren't they included in the meaning of the term 'person' [*adam*]?

The Gemara explains: *Indeed they are not.* As it is written: "And you my sheep, the sheep of my pasture, are people [*adam*]" (Ezekiel 34:31), from which it is derived that you, the Jewish people, are called *adam*, but Gentiles are not called *adam*.

Soferim 15,10: R. Simeon b. Yoḥai taught: *Kill the best of the heathens* [in time of war]; crush the brain of the best of serpents. The worthiest of women indulges in witchcraft. Happy is he who does the will of the Omnipresent.[7]

Sanhedrin 58b,7: For what reason did Adam not marry his daughter? So that Cain would marry his sister and they would procreate immediately, as it is stated: "Loving kindness will be built up forever" (Psalms 89:2).[8] This verse alludes to the fact that at the beginning of the world's existence, it was permitted for men to marry their sisters, which was later forbidden in the verse: "And if a man shall take his sister…it is a shameful

[7] Ed.: 'Soferim' is considered a "minor tractate" and thus not formally part of the Talmud, but it is still accepted as official Judaic teaching. The call to 'kill the best of the Gentiles' is especially troubling. The bracketed phrase "in time of war" is disputed; apparently it was added at a later date, to 'soften' the damning tone.

[8] According to the Talmudic tradition, a sister was born together with Cain, whom he then married; the children named in Genesis 4 then came from these two. Cf. Sanhedrin 32: "In the eighth hour [of the 6th day of creation] two [Adam and Eve] got into bed and four came down again." Similarly, in Midrash Berëschîth rabba, c. 22: "Rabbi Joshua ben Karcha said: 'Two got into bed and seven came down again'—Cain and his twin sister, as well as Abel and his twin sister." The human race thus perpetuates itself, because Adam mercifully left Cain's sister to be his wife and did not take her for himself.

thing" (Lev 20:17).[9] The Gemara infers: If it had not been so, if God had not specially permitted Cain to marry his sister, she would have been forbidden to him. This is difficult, according to the opinion of Rabbi Akiva, who deems it permitted for a Gentile to marry his sister.

58b,9: Rav Huna says: A Gentile is permitted to marry his daughter.[10] And if you say, for what reason did Adam not marry his daughter? It was so that Cain would marry his sister, because it is stated: "Loving kindness will be built up forever."

58b,10: And there are those who say that Rav Huna did not say this; rather, Rav Huna says: A Gentile is prohibited from marrying his daughter. Know that this is the *halakha,* as Adam did not marry his daughter.[11] The Gemara rejects this statement: But that is not so, as there, this is the reason Adam did not marry his daughter: So that Cain could marry his sister, because it is stated: "Loving kindness will be built up forever."

58b,11: Rav Ḥisda says: A Canaanite slave is permitted to marry his mother, and he is permitted to marry his daughter. This is because he has left the category of a Gentile by immersing in a ritual bath for the purpose of becoming a slave to a Jew, and consequently all his previous family relationships are disregarded. But he has not entered the category of a Jew, as evidenced by the fact that he is not obligated to observe all the *mitzvot* of male Jews. Therefore, the decree of the Sages prohibiting the maternal relatives of converts does not apply to him.

58b,17: Rabbi Ḥanina says: A Gentile who struck a Jew is liable to receive the death penalty, as it is stated when Moses saw an Egyptian striking a Hebrew: "And he turned this way and that way, and when he

---

[9] In the incest prohibitions in Leviticus 18, there is no prohibition of carnal contact between the father and his daughter!

[10] Ed.: Interesting that the rabbis allow incest (sister, daughter) among the Gentiles—with all the moral and genetic harm that this entails (genetic diseases from inbreeding, etc). It is almost as if they are happy to see the Gentiles degrade themselves. Lesson: be extremely wary when a Jew dictates to you your morals!

[11] Adam is not regarded as a Jew, but rather only Abraham from the time of his circumcision, during which God himself held his foreskin. As a non-Jew, according to the above thinking, Adam could indeed have taken his daughter as his wife! The evangelist Luke, who emphasizes *heathen Christianity*, therefore traces Jesus' family tree back to the "non-Jew" Adam, in contrast to the *Judeo-Christian* Matthew, who only goes back to Abraham.

saw that there was no one around, he killed the Egyptian and hid him in the sand" (Exodus 2:12).

58b,18: And Rabbi Ḥanina says: One who slaps the cheek of a Jew is considered as though he slapped the cheek of the Divine Presence…

58b,25: And Reish Lakish says: A Gentile who observed Sabbath is liable to receive the death penalty, as it is stated: "And day and night shall not cease" (Genesis 8:22), which literally means: 'And day and night they shall not rest.' This is interpreted to mean that the descendants of Noah may not take a day of rest. And the Master said that their prohibition is their death penalty, i.e., the punishment for any prohibition regarding descendants of Noah is execution. Ravina says: If a descendant of Noah observes a day of rest on *any* day of the week, even one not set aside for religious worship, e.g., on a Monday, he is liable to be killed.

Sanhedrin 59a,2: And Rabbi Yoḥanan says: A Gentile who engages in Torah study is liable to receive the death penalty.

APPENDIX B

Literature on the *Shulchan Aruch*

A. Translations

Complete Translations

Complete German translation by Heinrich Löwe.

a) "*Shulchan Aruch* or the Four Jewish Codes of Law." Translated by Heinrich Georg F. Löwe Sr. (Vol. I: Even Ha-ëser, Hamburg 1837; II: Choshen Mishpat, Hamburg 1838; III: Orach Chayim, Hamburg, 1839; IV: Yoreh De'ah, Hamburg, 1840.)

b) "*Shulchan Aruch* or the Four Jewish Codes of Law." Translated by Heinrich Georg F. Löwe Sr. (I: Orach Chayim and Jared dëah together with translations of Jewish prayers, translation of the 1st chapter of the Talmud Tractate Berachoth together with Gemara, digressions and parallel passages from the Palestinian Talmud. II: Choshen ha-mishapt and Eben Ha-ëser, translation of Jewish matrimonial forms and the 613 Jewish commandments and prohibitions). "Second Edition, Vienna 1896."

Only Karo's text of the *Shulchan Aruch* is translated, not the Hagahôth of Isserles, which is so important and makes the *Shulchan Aruch* complete (see above §10). Löwe's translation of the Orach Chayim is abridged and freely expressed, in part paraphrased, free likewise from the Yoreh De'ah and the Choshen Mishpat, which is free and abridged from the Even Ha'ezer. Löwe, a baptized Jew, wanted his translation to have an enlightening effect (and partly a missionary effect on the Jews). Löwe's translation is therefore primarily focused on the main content, less on accuracy in detail, and even less on good expression. The translation is therefore deficient in places, even erroneous. The second edition, edited by the Catholic non-specialist Prof. Dr. Joseph Deckert, has repeated some of Löwe's work, improved other parts, and made still others worse.

Total Translations in Summary

1. Spanish translation by Joseph Franco.

Schulchan hapanîm, libra llama do in Latino mesa de alma, per que es compuesto de todoa los dinim necessarios para el ombre, tresladado del libro del Gaon Joseph Karo. Venetiae 1602 apud Jo. de Gara (40, 187ff.).

Spanish in Hebrew letters. Only the most important things are briefly translated; the first part of the *Shulchan Aruch* (Orach Chayim) is considered the most important, next is the second (Yoreh De'ah). The book is obviously intended for the practical-ritual daily use by those Jews who are not sufficiently proficient in Hebrew. In the 17th century, Spanish was, so to speak, the world language and also the mother tongue of the "Sephardic" Jews expelled from Spain. Does the strange Latin phrase "table of the soul" indicate the use of a Latin summary in the *Shulchan Aruch*?

2. Spanish translation by Moses Altaras.

Libro de mantiemento de la alma, e nel qual se contiene el modo con que se a de regir el Judio en todos sus actiones, traduzido del hebraico al Spagnol per Mose Altaras. Con licencia dei Superiori, an 5369 Venetiae 1609 apud Belthasar. Bonibelli. (40, 175 pp.)

Pp. 1-104: Orach Chayim (all chapters but very abbreviated); 105-165: Yoreh De'ah (with selections and abbreviations); 165-169: Even Ha'ezer (very briefly the most necessary main points); 169-175: Choshen Mishpat (brief summary of contents).

The preference for the first two parts of the *Shulchan Aruch* proves the practical-ritual purpose of the translation, aimed at Jewish devotion to the laws in daily life. Altaras, like Franco (§17), has taken into account only Karo's text, not Isserles.

3. Selected German translation by Julius Dessauer.

"The Ritual Laws of the Israelites, edited from the sources of the Orach Chayim, Yoreh De'ah, Even Ha'ezer and Choshen Mishpat. With punctuation of the text and German translation, together with explanatory additions and notes, edited by Julius Dessauer." 2 Parts. Ofen. 1868/69.

Part I (1868) comprises 237 pages, texts, and translations together with explanations from Orach Chayim alone, Part II (1869) likewise from the other three parts. The purpose for use in the daily religious-legal life clearly emerges here as well. The selection of texts is already very scant in Part I, even more so in Part II. The translation allows itself some liberties.

4. Selected German translation by Philipp Lederer.

"*Shulchan Aruch.* The religious statutes, regulations, customs, and traditions of Judaism.... Edited and arranged for the first time according to the sources by Philipp Lederer." 4 Parts/Pressburg (Pilsen) 1897 ff.

The excerpts from the four parts of the *Shulchan Aruch* are rather insufficiently translated and explained. Part I is intended "for the synagogue, school and home". Part II "for use as a handbook by rabbis, teachers, cantors, community officials and synagogue presidents." Thus, the work seems to pass on scientific value from the outset; as such, it does not have much merit.

5. Selected French translation by "Jean de Pavly".

"*Rituel du judaisme. Traduit pour la première fois sur l'original chaldéo-rabbinique et accompagné de notes et remarques de tous les commentateurs. Par Jean de Pavly. Avec le concours de M. A. Neviasky.*" Tome I-IV. Orléans 1897-99.

Part I (1897) comprises V parts and 32 pages, Part II (1898) 170, Part III (1898) 144, Part IV (1899) 98 pages. Only Karo is included, not Isserles. The translation of the text excerpts as well as the remarks of "all commentators" are equally insufficient. The whole text is a promulgated hoax, "Jean de Pavly" here (in contrast to those mentioned below §26) is the code name for a brazen ignoramus.

Translations of Particular Portions

1. Selected translations in French from Even Ha'ezer.

"*Code Rabbinique Eben Haëser traduit par extraits avec les explications des docteurs juifs, la jurisprudence de la cour d'Alger et des notes comparatives de droit français et de droit musulman par E. Sautayra, président du tribunal de Mostagenem, et M. Charleville, grand-rabbin de la province d'Oran.*" Paris-Alger. Tome I 1868; II 1869.

Part I: pp. 7-12 Preface; 13-36 Introduction (History of Jewish law, except for Karo); 39-172 French translation (in excerpt) and explanation (in the footnotes) of the first two sections of Even Ha'ezer; 175-183. Part II: pp. 5-354 Translation and explanation (as above) of the last three chapters; 355-360 Contents. By Senate resolution of July 14, 1865, the Jews of Algeria were permitted to handle civil disputes among themselves according to their religious laws.

2. German translation of Choshen Mishpat. ("Dr. J. de Pavly.")

"Choshen Mishpat, or the Civil and Criminal Law of the Jews. For the first time freely translated from the original into German and provided with sources, explanations, and the most important remarks of the commentaries by Dr. J. de Pavly, Professor at the Collège du Sacré-Cour in Lyon." St. Ludwig im Elsass, published by Alphonse Besserer. 1893.

Page cf.: Table of Contents; VII-XXIII: Preface; 1-171: German translation of the main content of all paragraphs of Choshen Mishpat with very brief footnotes, which are just as insufficient as the translation. Only Karo's text is considered, Isserle's is not. The translation is only an inadequate summary of what the translator considers to be the "main content" of the individual paragraphs, and is written in miserable non-German: P. XIII "misunderstood" (misjudged), "grasped by the roots" (strapped), "throughout the existence"'; P. 7 "the member"; P. 11 "the party, etc." All the inconvenient texts are suppressed, from the commentaries only the location without the text and no indication of the content is offered, in fatuous abbreviations. A "Dr. J. de Pavly" has never been a professor in Lyon. This "Dr. J. de Pavly" has certainly nothing to do with the Dr. Johannes A.F.E.L.V. von Pavly", mentioned below (§ 26), but rather with the "Dr. J. de Pavly", mentioned above (§ 21), and the "Dr. J. de Pavly", mentioned in the same way. Most strange is, that this "de Pavly", with no words, makes mention of his own predecessor, "Johannes...von Pavly".

Translations of Extended Excerpts

1. Latin translation of the Choshen Mishpat.

"*Sententiae Rabbinorum de successione ab intestato et testamentaria collectae a R. Joseph Karo ... in libro Shulchan Aruch dicto, per R. Mosen Isserles emandato atque suppleto. In Linguam latinam vertit et passim illustravit Christian Gottlob Meyer, SS.Th.Stud.*" Halle 1775.

P. I-XXVIII: Foreword, Preface, Table of Contents; 1-117: Latin translations of Choshen Mishpat 276-289 in 14 chapters, together with numerous notes; 119-149: German translations of a Hebrew Testament, two rabbinical reports and a decree on Guardianship on the occasion of this Testament; 150-163: Subject Index; 164: Misprints. The studious manuscript can be found at the Leipzig University Library, among other places.

2. German translations of Yoreh De'ah 240-284.

"The Schulchan-Aruch. Translated by Ignaz W. Bak." Budapest 1884.

The title is misleading. It consists of only §§ 240-284 of the 403 paragraphs of the Schulchan-*Aruch*, and part of Yoreh De'ah, which are unremarkably translated.

3. German translation of Orach Chayim 1-160. ("Dr. John A.F.E.L.V. von Pavly.")

"*Shulchan Aruch* (Set Table, Ezekiel 23:41) or the Ritual and Law book of Judaism, consisting of the following four parts: 1. Orach Chayim (Path of Life, Psalms 16:10), 2. Yoreh De'ah (Teachings of Wisdom, Isaiah 28:9), 3. Choshen Mishpat (Breastplate of Judgment, 2 Moses 28:15), 4. Eben ëser (Victory stone, 1 Sam. 7:12). For the first time freely translated from the original into German and provided with sources, explanations, and the most important remarks from all commentaries, by Dr. Johannes A.F.E.L.V. von Pavly, with the assistance of outstanding scholars." Basel, published by Stephan Marugg. Debit commission for the book trade: Verlags-Magazin (I. Schabelitz) in Zürich. 1888.

Only four installments have appeared (at 4 months.) Pages 9-38: Table of contents of the 697 paragraphs of the Orach Chayim; 39-640 German Translation of O. Ch 1-160, 12 with notes. The translation also provides the Hagahôth of Isserles. Correctly, Prof. Gildemeister-Bonn assesses it as follows: "I…find it consistently reliable and good. Also the explanations and excerpts from the commentaries valuable and in proper measure. It astonishes me that the translation calls itself 'free' on the title, …since it is in fact a literal and faithful one," etc.

Translations of Individual Passages

1. Eisenmenger's Quotes with German translations.

Johannes Andreas Eisenmenger[1] lists, in his work *Entdecktes Judenthum* ("Judaism Uncovered"), (2 Vols., Frankfurt a. M. 1700; reprint Königsberg 1711), many passages from the *Shulchan Aruch* in the original text with German translation.[2]

---

[1] Born in 1654 in Mannheim, died 20 December 1704. As a professor in Heidelberg, he studied Judaism and its literature in Amsterdam and had more knowledge of it than all of today's Jewish and Christian scholars combined. Before his countless translations, he almost always offers the original text of the often very rare Jewish works he uses, and only very rarely does he have a translation that is not entirely flawless. When Jewish scribblers today describe his two thick quarto volumes as a "slander tomes," they don't even know how stupid they are. As is well known, the 1st edition (1700), after Eisenmenger had refused a Jewish offer of 10,000 talers to refrain from printing it, was confiscated by the emperor at the instigation of the Frankfurt Jews (only released in 1740), whereupon Frederick I of Prussia had the book reprinted at his own expense in Königsberg in 1711, where the emperor had nothing to say, and bestowed the edition on Eisenmenger's heirs.

[2] a) Orach Chayim 690 (Eisenmenger II 170).

b) Yoreh De'ah 2, 1 (II 616); 113, 1 (II 628); 116,5 (II 644); 117,1 (II 632f.); 119,8 (II 643); 124,4 (II 626); 124,6 (II 620f.); 125,1 (II 627); 141,1 Hagah (I 531); 148,1 (I 562); 151,14 (I 616); 154 (nicht: 124), 1 f. (II 626, vgl.

Eisenmenger translates according to the 1661 Amsterdam small octavo edition of the *Shulchan Aruch*. Where this volume offers "Goy", he retains "Goy"; where he finds "Nochri" (heathen) in the text, he correctly translates as "Foreigner"; wherever *Akum* is there, he always translates it as "worshippers of idols and constellations". Only in his explanations of such passages does he declare that they refer "also" or generally to Christians, but he admits that the Christian are not alone in being named *Akum*.

2. Paraphrases of passages from the *Shulchan Aruch* in the "*Judenspiegel*".

a) "*Judenspiegel* (Jewish Mirror) or 100 Jewish Laws, newly revealed, still valid today, regarding dealings by Jews with the Christians, with a highly interesting introduction depicting the origin and development of Jewish Law. By Dr. Justus, *speculi opifex in lumine veritatis*." Paderborn 1883.

The author is the notorious Ahron Briman, a Jew who first became a Protestant, then a Catholic. About him, compare my writings, "*Rabbi und Diakonus*", Leipzig 1922, especially p. 21ff., and "*Rabbinische Fabeln*", ibid., 1922, p. 100; furthermore Strack, "*Das Blut*" etc., (5th-7th editions, Münich 1900).

In the first four editions, "Justus"-Briman offers no actual translations, but instead more paraphrases of passages taken from the *Shulchan Aruch* with tendentious additions. Only in the 5th edition are the genuinely translated sentences of the *Shulchan Aruch* distinguished from Briman's additions by quotation marks.

The 5th edition contains: pp. 5-38 Preface (with many inaccuracies, generally insufficient); pp. 39-700 the 100 so-called "Laws" in German translation together with notes; pp. 98-102 a misguided excursus on the Blood Ritual; pp. 102-111 appendix (replies to the criticisms, shallow and misleading); pp. 111ff. final remarks on Pavly's translation.

I 613); 155,1 (II 228); 158,1 (II 189f., 229f.); 160,2 ((II 599); 228,1 (II 492); 232,14 and Hagah (II 510ff.); 254,1 (I 617); 334,43 (I 332f., II 479).

c) Choshen ha-mischpat 25 and Hagah (II 478f.); 26,1 and Hagah (II 472); 28,3 (II 479); 34.19 (I 615); 87,20 and Hagah (II 514f.); 95,1 Beër ha-golah (II 578); 228,6 (II 630); 231,1 (II 575); 348 Hagah (II 579f.); 348,3 and 359,1 (II 585); 425,5 Beër ha-golah (II 90f.).

The book is useless. Its only significance lies in the fact that for a long time it directed public attention again toward the *Shulchan Aruch*, and in conjunction with the Paderborn "*Judenspiegel*" trial of December 10, 1883 gave impetus to the more recent literature on the *Shulchan Aruch*.

3. Ecker's Quotations with German Translation.

"*Der Judenspiegel*" in the Light of Truth. A scientific investigation by Dr. Jakov Ecker[3], Professor for Semitic Philosophy at the Royal Academy of Münster." Paderborn (März) 1884. (Second improved and expanded edition. Paderborn [April] 1884.)

For the passages of the *Shulchan Aruch* quoted by "Justus"-Briman, Ecker offers the basic Hebrew text together with his own generally correct translations and explanatory notes. Some of his justifications of the "*Judenspiegel*" seem rather bold; also, in his introduction some things are incorrect; he is especially unclear about "*Akum*". If one considers how, back in the early eighties, even the "great lights of the church" were with respect to Rabbinical matters, Ecker's book may at least be considered a noteworthy achievement.

4. Others.

Translations (or at least summaries) of individual paragraphs of the *Shulchan Aruch* also appear frequently in all kinds of works, e.g. from earlier times in Buxtorf's *Synagoga judaica* (Basel 1643 er al.), *De sponsalibus ac divortiis* (again 1652 and 1662), Selden's *Uxor hebraica* (Frankfurt a.M 1673) and in other works; from more recent times e.g. in Hoffmann's and Marx-Dalman's writings mentioned above (under sections 2 and 3), in my "Rabbinic Fables" and in Fiebig's "*Jews and non-Jews*" (Leipzig 1922, Translation mostly correct, even though un-German, explanations as a rule apologetic toward the Jews). And further, in Theodor Fritsch's book "*The Conflict about God and Talmud*", Leipzig 1922, etc.

---

[3] Born on 27 February 1851 in Lisdorf, died in 1912 as a highly respected professor at the Episcopal Seminary in Trier. For more about him and the outrageous defamation of the dead man by the Weimar state rabbi Dr. Wiesen and (now Dr.) Fiebig from Leipzig, see my writing "*Rabbi und Diakonus*" ("Rabbi and Deacon") Leipzig 1922.

The translation and explanations of passages of the *Shulchan Aruch* in the pamphlets of the "Central Association of German Citizens of the Jewish Faith" I have criticized in my "*Rabbinical Fables*."

B. Writings on the *Shulchan Aruch*

Of course, it cannot fall to me to list every little writing that mentions the *Shulchan Aruch*. I am mainly interested in informing readers about the writings that have appeared since the *Shulchan Aruch* controversy of 1884, and have acquired a certain meaning in the further progress of this controversy.

Of the articles on the *Shulchan Aruch* found in encyclopedias, only Dalman's in the "Real Encyclopedia for Protestant Theology and the Church", is really useful, while, for example, what Hamburger offers in his "Real Encyclopedia of Judaism" is completely unsuitable. The encyclopedias in foreign languages offer nothing new.

What is said in the introduction to the translations of Meyer, Löwe, Sautayra-Charleville, "*Judenspiegel*," and Ecker, does not suffice, nor do the brief notes by Z. Frankel (*The Judicial Proof for Mosaic-Talmudic Law*, Berlin 1846, P. 108f.), M. Jost (*History of Judaism and its Sects*, Leipzig Bk. III, 1851, p. 129, 454), H. Graetz (*History of the Israelites*[4], G. Karpeles (*History of Jewish Literature*, Berlin 1886, Bk. II 971), H. Ellenberger, (*Historical Handbook*, Budapest 1883, p. 407) etc. I treat, thus, only the most important.

Literature Since 1884 (through 1929)

1 Johann Gildemeister (1812-90, Prof. at Bonn): "The *Shulchan Aruch*, A Judicially demanded Report." Bonn 1884. Still worth read-

[4] Graetz, *History of the Israelites*, Book IX, Second Ed. 1877, p. 414f.: "Karo gave his work the character of a book of laws ... Karo's codex was immediately received with joy, disseminated and recognized as an inviolable norm from then until the end of the 18th century almost without contradiction, and is still largely decisive now." P. 133: "To this day, the decisions [of the *Schulchan Aruch*] form for [Orthodox] German and Polish Jews and whatever pertains to them, the religious norm, the official Judaism."

ing in part today, though some errors. (Main adversary: D. Hoffmann, see below 3.)

2 Manuel Joel (Prof. at Breslau): "Against Gildemeister." Breslau 1884 (Most unseemly tone.)

3 D. Hoffmann (Lecturer at the Rabbinical Seminary in Berlin): "The *Shulchan Aruch* and the Rabbis on the relations of the Jews to those of different faiths." First Edition Berlin 1885, p. 149; Second Edition Berlin 1894.) Hoffmann brings lots of material from the standpoint of Orthodox Judaism, corrects errors, e.g. Briman's and Ecker's, but proceeds quite one-sidedly, apologetic for Judaism.[5]

---

[5] In contrast to the "*Judenspiegel*" of Dr. Justus (Briman), Hoffmann has compiled a "Genuine Judenspiegel"—see above § 28, on pp. 80-108 of his writing "*Der Schulchan Aruch*"—which in its 111 paragraphs is supposed to represent, so to speak, a small *Schulchan Aruch* in the vest pocket. The credulous, non-expert reader naturally thinks that what Hoffman says is all correctly and honestly taken from the *Schulchan Aruch*. And at most, Hoffmann, as an orthodox Jewish scholar (who defends the *Schulchan Aruch* as far as possible), has only picked out from it the "raisins", and has omitted from his compilation the evil "bitter almonds", although these must belong to any "genuine" compendium. So it is, except that Hoffmann, in his apologetic overzealousness, offers the reader not only the "raisins" of the *Schulchan Aruch*, but also all sorts of other sweets, which do not come from the *Schulchan Aruch*, but from other works!

Old Johann Andreas Eisenmenger, who wrote his "Judaism Uncovered" more than 235 years ago, has been accused of having "uncritically" treated the most diverse Jewish writings as equal, regardless of whether he encounters the Talmud, the *Schulchan Aruch*, the writings of Maimonides, or some remote Kabbalistic writings and the like. But apart from the fact that in Eisenmenger's time one did not yet know the current critical separation of sources, one maliciously forgets that Eisenmenger is by no means writing a systematic and critical "Theology of Judaism" or something similar, but rather he only wants to compile from Jewish writings a "thorough and truthful account" of the many 'terrible' blasphemies against the Trinity, the New Testament, etc., and also from the same sources the religious and theological errors "as well as many ridiculous and entertaining fables and other nonsensical things." So, he wanted to give a general characterization of Judaism or the Jewish spirit, and he could find it in all books of post-Biblical literature (as an Orthodox Jew, he has a religious respect for the Old Testament), indeed, even if he saw the worst in it. From his intimate dealings with them, he knew especially the downsides of the Jews and their literature; moreover, the Jews were still in their Middle Ages at that time, differed little in their views from the Talmudic rabbis, and, by the way, quoted authorities from the most diverse centuries just as confusingly and colorfully as it happens, for example, in the Talmud itself.

Incidentally, Eisenmenger is also fair enough to defend the Jews against the accusation that their writings prescribe ritual murder, the "Kol nidré", intentional perjury, etc., and also to cite and examine in detail opposing opinions against what he has put forward. He also frequently quotes from later sources, for example, from the Talmud, etc., which he could have substantiated.

Thusly, the "unscientific" Eisenmenger! But now Dr. D. Hoffmann, who wants to be a representative of today's "Science of Judaism"! What about his "Genuine Judenspiegel"? Instead of reproducing my own judgment, I quote Marx-Dahlman's equally calm and devastating words (*Jüdisches Fremdenrecht* (Jewish Law on Foreigners) Karlsruhe ad Leipzig, P. 58):

> A false impression is created by the fact that [Hoffmann's] 'Genuine Judenspiegel', after the introductory words, is supposed to represent the *Schulchan Aruch*, whereas it contains sentences which were actually pronounced by later rabbis, which do not correspond to the meaning of the *Schulchan Aruch* itself.(!) One falsehood is the assertion that "every conscientious Jew must observe whatever is in the 'Genuine Judenspiegel'" as though required by religious law, so that this collection of laws [Hoffmann's] could be incorporated into every Jewish religious book.
>
> No, Hoffmann's *Judenspiegel* not only includes quotations which (because they come from old books on morality) cannot claim full 'religious-legal' significance: it also treats the words of the commentators of the *Schulchan Aruch* as equivalent to its own statements. Although Hoffmann must be aware, for example, that Moses Ribkas by no means enjoys the same recognition everywhere as the actual *Schulchan Aruch* with the addition of Isserles (Hagahôth, see above § 10).
>
> The reader is completely deceived if the [allegedly genuine] Judenspiegel communicates from the *Schulchan Aruch* only what is suitable to awaken a favorable prejudice in favorable light, but carefully conceals everything else. Had the Israel of the *Schulchan Aruch* really been the 'salutary messenger of peace even among the worst heathens', as when Hoffmann praises it in chapter VII—the fact that this 'Peace messenger' aroused hatred wherever it appeared is one of the most inexplicable mysteries in the history of the world.

So arousing a false appearance, an untruth, a deception and on top of that (ibid., p. 45), Dalman accuses the Jewish lecturer at the Rabbinical Seminary in Berlin and author of the "*Echte Judenspiegel*" of dishonest proceedings", and Hoffmann, who is otherwise so lavish in swear words (swindle, forgery, dastard, fraud, liar, shameless, etc.) takes this lying down or meekly replies

4 M. L. Rodkinssohn: "The *Shulchan Aruch* in Relation to Jews and Christians." Vienna 1884, 68 pages. Reformed Jewish standpoint, even a rejection of the *Shulchan Aruch*; however, his critique of Jewish Orthodoxy, of "Justus", Ecker, and Hoffman are uniformly lacking in expertise.
5 J. Goldschmidt (District Rabbi in Weilburg): articles in No 34-46 of the "Israelite Weekly" of 1884. Unfair, completely inadequate, even close to dishonest.
6 Adolf Lewin (Rabbi in Koblenz): "Der Judenspiegel of Justus". Magdeburg 1884, 89 pp. (Even worse than Goldschmidt.)
7 Moritz Baum: "An Important Chapter" etc.; 2nd Improved Edition, Frankfurt a.M. 1884. (The first 48 pages will prove that "the Christians and such peoples" were not already called "Akûm, Goy, Nochri" in the Talmud, let alone later, which is nonsense. The second 11 pages give a good report on the "Judenspiegel" trial in Münster [December 10, 1883] with forays against the experts, Prof. Ecker and especially Treu, the Jewish Seminary Lecturer.)
8 Gustaf (Marx) Dalman (now Professor at Greifswald): "Jewish Foreign Law, anti-Semitic polemic and Jewish apologetics." Karlsruhe and Leipzig 1886, 80 pp. (pp.1-40 Criticisms of Briman and Ecker; 41-78 of Hoffmann, Goldschmidt, Lewin, Rodkinssohn, etc. The best and most factual of all the previous writings on the *Shulchan Aruch*, especially from p. 41 onward. Unfortunately, it has long been out of print in the book trade and, strangely, has never been reprinted, although the Institutum Judaicum in Berlin, among whose writings this book was the first, would long since have had the duty to see to a new edition!

---

with an embarrassed irrelevance. It doesn't help; Dalman's accusation (ibid., p. 57) stays with him forever:

"Through concealment, distortion and silence [by Hoffmann], the culpability of the past of Judaism is consistently removed from its image." The judgment of such an honest friend of the Jews (and indeed, a friend to millions of Jews), such an excellent connoisseur of the Talmudic-Rabbinic literature, and on top of that the author of the best Aramaic grammar, etc., as Professor D. Gustav Dalman is, may be called, with full justification, a death sentence for Hoffmann's apologetic artifices.

9 Bernard Fischer (Rabbi, 1821-1906): "Talmud and *Shulchan Aruch*", pp. 2-10, 6ff. Leipzig 1892, 111 pages. (Long out of print, presently partly outdated, many interesting details, yet various errors.)
10 Paul Förster (School professor): "Talmud and *Shulchan Aruch*." Breslau 1892, 58 pages. (A lecture; unscientific and full of errors; the texts reproduced and treated without understanding, according to the first editions of Briman-Justus' "*Judenspiegel*").
11 "Why the noise?" Letter by a Teuton to his fellow 'Citizens' of the Semitic Race", pp. 34-47. (Antisemitic pamphlet.)
12 R. Königsberger in "Israelite Weekly" from December 9, 1893. (Unauthorized.)
13 August Wünsche (titular professor, retired girls' school rector in Dresden): "Are the Christians to be regarded as 'Akûm' (idolaters) according to the religious-legal writings of the Jews?" Supplement to the München-Augsburger Allgemeine Zeitung 1893, No. 53, p. 1 (One-sidedly apologetic and in many cases as inaccurate, as everything that Wünsche writes.)
14 F. E. v. Langen: "The Jewish Secret Law and German state representation." Leipzig 1895, VI and 114 pages. (Discusses the *Shulchan Aruch*, especially on pp. 29, 34-51, 66-75, giving very interesting information about the "Kitzur *Shulchan Aruch*" and the history of the deadlocked German translation of the *Shulchan Aruch* of "Dr. Johannes von Pavly", likewise about the translations of this or the other "de Pavly". Otherwise strongly polemical.)
15 Ch. Tschernowitz: "The Origin of the *Shulchan Aruch*." Bern 1915, 79 pages. (Scientific, but inarticulate style, numerous errata, unclear presentation).
16 Theodor Fritsch: "The Controversy between God and Talmud." Leipzig 1922, 94 pages (pp. 64f. accurate polemic against the judgments of the Leipzig Pastor, Lecturer, etc., D. Paul Fiebig on the *Shulchan Aruch*.)
17 Erich Bischoff: "Rabbinical Fables. A forensic report." Leipzig 1922, 108 pages. (Impartial; correction of many erroneous Jewish translations and judgments).
18 Simon Bernfeld: "Jewish Business Ethics according to the Talmud and *Shulchan Aruch*." Berlin 1924, 28 pp. (Apologetic, all kinds of

quotes, mostly from the Mishnèh thorah of Maimonides, from the *Shulchan Aruch* only a few short important passages on p. 20ff.)

19 E. Munk: Spurious Talmud Quotations. Berlin 1924. (Apparently—according to the Preface—an expanded pamphlet of the "Central Association of German Citizens of the Jewish Faith" and like most of these, cursory, erroneous, and scientifically worthless. Although Hoffmann and Fiebig are written out "in part literally". The treatment of the two simply quoted *Shulchan Aruch* passages is student-like).

C. The *Kitzur Shulchan Aruch*

This work constitutes a practical abstract from the full *Shulchan Aruch.*

Kitzur *Shulchan Aruch* ha-schalêm ("Excerpted from the entire *Shulchan Aruch.*") By Salomo Ganzfried, Rabbinate Professor from Hungary. (2nd ed. 1866) New edition with 3 commentaries, 2 parts. Vilna 1901.

Marx-Dalman used the 14th (!) edition of this book, which since 1866 had to be reprinted until then no less than 13 times (i.e. within 18 years)— a proof of its strong circulation! As Marx-Dalman correctly remarks, Ganzfried's "Kitzur" wants to be a detailed excerpt from the *Shulchan Aruch*, but "only complies what is unavoidably necessary for the practice of daily life." And as "unavoidably necessary", it seems to the "Kitzur" to reproduce regulations from the *Shulchan Aruch*, which, in Ganzfried's manner of compilation, can only be related to Christians!

> In Chapter 167 (of the "Kitzur"), dealing with idolatry are mentioned as idolatrous things forbidden for use: Idols (the images and crosses in the churches and along the roads), their ornaments, censers, chalices and musical instruments. For the Houses of Idols (Churches), not even windows are allowed to be made. The idolaters are not allowed to sell books that are necessary for the idolatry, nor are they allowed to sell Bible editions that they have falsified. (!) The chanting and singing, that comes from a House of Idols, and the smells (of incense, etc.) should be avoided. The otherwise forbidden mockery may be used against idolatry. Giving something to 'Idolaters', without being sure of

> something in return on their part, is forbidden. One must not praise them either. Because they are suspected of murder, one may not be alone with them. An Israelite woman may only nurse the child of a 'pagan' she knows, because otherwise there would be fear of enmity. One must not cause the 'pagan' to speak the name of the idols. Only in the case of an oath prompted by business relations with pagans is an exception permitted. When one sees the house of an 'idolator,' one should say: 'The house of the proud, the Lord will pull down' (Proverbs 15:25)!

For the Rabbinical apologist D. Hoffmann, it was very unpleasant to see here the proof that the "Kitzur"—this practical Rabbinical school book—regarded Christianity as idolatry. He had a letter written to the elderly Ganzfried, that he did not want "the goyim(!), under whose shadow we shelter" to be considered idolaters. But Marx-Dalman dismisses him impressively (and yet, much too mildly) in the following way:

> If, in that chapter 167 [of the "Kitzur"] one wanted to let it be debatable in the beginning, whether to the cups, censers, temples, garments and lights of the idolaters, are to be reckoned the Christian ones, so it is said under no. 5 [of ch. 167] without further introduction: 'The image of the cross, which they' (obviously the idolaters mentioned above) 'worship, is forbidden.' When then in No. 6, there is talk of 'adulterated Bibles' of the Old Testament, which may not be sold to them any more than other things connected with 'idolatry'; when in No. 11, places are mentioned where the 'idolaters' gather to obtain forgiveness for sins, it is clear that the writer of the chapter is not thinking merely of negroes and Indians. Throughout the chapter, there is no trace of a distinction to discover between idolaters and Christians.

—according to Marx-Dalman.[6]

---

[6] He very correctly (p. 72) refers to the ritual legal opinion ("*Theshubôth*") of the modern rabbi Joseph Schwarz of Jerusalem (p. 114ff.), where it is decided that only the crucifixes in the church are to be regarded as "idols" in the full

Until 1892/93, this "Kitzur *Shulchan Aruch*" was also in use in some places of Jewish religious education in Germany! When this was pointed out at the time, a commission of unprofessional theologians was appointed in Prussia, which came to the bright conclusion that the "*Shulchan Aruch* would be used in no public or private elementary school", that is to say, in any Jewish religious education. However, the "*Berliner Börsencourier*" of 30 September 1893 gleefully mocked the strangeness of this enunciation, rightly remarking that it was about the "Kitzur" and not the *Shulchan Aruch* itself, and that government statement is about as wise as saying that the *Corpus juris* is not taught in schools. To what extent the "Kitzur" has been used in the religious instruction of Orthodox Jewish Schools in Prussia, nobody knows even today. In fact, it was used "in all classes" (i.e. from the 10th year of life on) of the Jewish Preparatory for teachers at Burgreppach still in 1891/92. And it was used in "a Baden commercial school" [!] in 1893, where its use was forbidden by the Baden Grand-Ducal Councilor of the Jews, because, among other things, "those passages that allow less humane behavior towards the idolatrous pagan must be identified as outdated and contradictory to today's refined conception of Judaism".[7] (*Karlruher Zeitung*, 17 July 1894.) Therefore,

---

sense of the word because they alone are venerated through worship. "For there [in the 'House of folly' (*Bëth thiphlah* instead of *Bëth thephillah* "House of Prayer")] is the site of the actual idol of the cross." According to Maimonides, the great Jewish teacher of the law, "the Christians are considered idolaters in every respect" (Marx-Dalman, p. 49), to Karo, the author of the *Shulchan Aruch*, at least in various respects (ibid., p. 51), and when Moses of Coucy (p. 70), in the section dealing with idolatry, speaks readily of chalices, wax candles and robes used in idolatry, further of Nital (Christmas) and Kèssach (Easter) as the "principle festivals of the idolaters", so does he mean only the Christians! See B. Fischer (*Talmud und Schulchan Aruch*, p. 6): "Ask even today the Christian citizen of England his fellow citizen of Jewish denomination who is meant by the "*Akum*" [idolater] of the *Shulchan Aruch*, and he will hear the truth that it is the Christian." Ganzfried's excuse that "the goyim under whose shadow we find ourselves" do not count to him as idolaters is a timid evasion and subterfuge, which the *Shulchan Aruch* commentary "Beér ha-golah" and the Paris Sanhedrin under Napoleon I had already demonstrated to him, for example, by the latter declaring that it did not consider the French Christians to be pagans, while asking this question regarding non-French Christians!

[7] "The idolaters are not human beings, they stand outside the law. Their lives need not be spared, their property is to be regarded as ownerless" etc., says

the "Upper Council" came to the conclusion "that the 'Kitzur *Shulchan Aruch*' is not suitable as a textbook."

Today [in 1929], the "Kitzur *Shulchan Aruch*" is again in use in Jewish religious schools. In Leipzig, it is for sale in three editions and in a German translation in the Jewish bookstore M. Kaufmann.

Chief Rabbi Fassel, *Die Mosaisch-Rabbinische Tugend- und Rechtslehre* (The Mosaic-Rabbinic Code of Virtue and Law) 2nd ed., p. 187.

Milton Keynes UK
Ingram Content Group UK Ltd.
UKHW051727231123
433139UK00020B/260